September 15, 2016

Dear Colleagues:

Last September, President Obama issued an Executive Order directing Federal agencies to integrate behavioral-science insights—research insights about how people make decisions and act on them—into the design of their policies and programs. The Executive Order also charged the Social and Behavioral Sciences Team (SBST), a cross-agency group of applied behavioral scientists, program officials, and policymakers, with providing policy guidance and advice to Federal agencies in support of this directive.

The *Social and Behavioral Sciences Team 2016 Annual Report* highlights SBST's progress implementing the President's directive over the past year in eight key policy areas: promoting retirement security, advancing economic opportunity, improving college access and affordability, responding to climate change, supporting criminal-justice reform, assisting job seekers, helping families get health coverage and stay healthy, and improving the effectiveness and efficiency of Federal Government operations. This report builds on SBST's 2015 report, which detailed over a dozen projects that helped more service members save for retirement, more students go to college and better manage their student loans, more veterans access education and career counseling benefits, and more family farmers gain access to credit.

As discussed in this report, SBST has turned its attention to some of the most important policy challenges facing the Nation, such as ensuring access to healthcare coverage for the millions of Americans who still lack it, expanding economic opportunity for workers and their families, and reducing carbon emissions to protect the planet. SBST has also applied a behavioral perspective to helping to keep families in Flint, Michigan safe from lead in water and helping communities across the Nation implement the recommendations of the President's Task Force on 21st Century Policing.

As part of addressing this diverse set of challenges, SBST has had to apply behavioral insights to an ever broader range of program features: from changing how programs communicate with individuals, to modifying the way programs are administered, to informing the design of policy.

I look forward to seeing a continuing stream of positive results, in the years ahead, building on the impressive work accomplished in SBST's first 2 years.

Sincerely,

John P. Holdren

John P. Holdren

Assistant to the President for Science and Technology
Director, Office of Science and Technology Policy

About the National Science and Technology Council

The National Science and Technology Council (NSTC) is the principal means by which the Executive Branch coordinates science and technology policy across the diverse entities that make up the Federal research and development (R&D) enterprise. One of the NSTC's primary objectives is establishing clear national goals for Federal science and technology investments. The NSTC prepares R&D packages aimed at accomplishing multiple national goals. The NSTC's work is organized under five committees: Environment, Natural Resources, and Sustainability; Homeland and National Security; Science, Technology, Engineering, and Mathematics (STEM) Education; Science; and Technology. Each of these committees oversees subcommittees and working groups that are focused on different aspects of science and technology. More information is available at www.whitehouse.gov/ostp/nstc.

About the Office of Science and Technology Policy

The Office of Science and Technology Policy (OSTP) was established by the National Science and Technology Policy, Organization, and Priorities Act of 1976. OSTP's responsibilities include advising the President in policy formulation and budget development on questions in which science and technology are important elements; articulating the President's science and technology policy and programs; and fostering strong partnerships among Federal, state, and local governments, and the scientific communities in industry and academia. The Director of OSTP also serves as Assistant to the President for Science and Technology and manages the NSTC. More information is available at www.whitehouse.gov/ostp.

About the Subcommittee on the Social and Behavioral Sciences Team

The Subcommittee on the Social and Behavioral Sciences Team (SBST) contributes to the activities of NSTC's Committee on Technology (CoT). SBST's purpose is to coordinate the application of social and behavioral science research to help Federal agencies advance their policy and program goals and better serve the Nation. SBST works to identify opportunities for Federal agencies to leverage social and behavioral science insights to advance the goals of their policies and programs, demonstrate the impact of these applications, and build capacity for applications of social and behavioral science across Federal agencies.

About this Document

This document was developed by the Subcommittee on the Social and Behavioral Sciences Team. The document was published by OSTP.

Copyright Information

This document is a work of the United States Government and is in the public domain (see 17 U.S.C. §105). Subject to the stipulations below, it may be distributed and copied with acknowledgement to OSTP. Copyrights to graphics included in this document are reserved by the original copyright holders or their assignees and are used here under the government's license and by permission. Requests to use any images must be made to the provider identified in the image credits or to OSTP if no provider is identified.

Printed in the United States of America, September 2016.

Acknowledgements

Many individuals across the Federal Government contributed to this report and the work it describes. Above all, none of the program improvements described here would have been possible without the creativity and diligence of the agency and program staff who collaborated on this work.

Particular recognition also goes to the General Services Administration's (GSA) Office of Evaluation Sciences (OES). Individuals on staff, on detail, or through a fellowship dedicated their technical expertise to complete many of the projects highlighted in this report. These team members include: Kelly Bidwell, Jacob Bowers, Hyunsoo Chang, Amira Choueiki, Juan Manuel Contreras, William Congdon, Michael DiDomenico, Lori Foster, Crystal Hall, Michael Hand, Nathaniel Higgins, Tatiana Homonoff, Zhanrui Kuang, Matthew Nagler, Daniel Shephard, Elana Safran, Will Tucker, and David Yokum. SBST and OES are also fortunate to draw on an outstanding network of academic collaborators, who contributed in numerous ways to the content of this report.

Additionally, SBST wishes to thank the leadership of GSA for their support of OES and SBST, with special thanks due to Adam Neufeld, Troy Cribb, Giancarlo Brizzi, Jon Clinton, and the broader Office of Government-wide Policy team for their ongoing efforts. SBST is grateful to Andy Black for his work designing this report.

And finally, SBST would like to thank Tom Kalil, Kumar Garg, and Meredith Drosback for their continued support of the team and help with this report.

NATIONAL SCIENCE AND TECHNOLOGY COUNCIL
COMMITTEE ON TECHNOLOGY
SUBCOMMITTEE ON THE SOCIAL AND BEHAVIORAL SCIENCES TEAM

National Science and Technology Council

Chair

John P. Holdren

Assistant to the President for Science
and Technology and Director,
Office of Science and Technology Policy

Staff

Afua Bruce

Executive Director
Office of Science and Technology Policy

Committee on Technology

Chair

Thomas Kalil

Deputy Director for Technology and Innovation
Office of Science and Technology Policy

Staff

Lusine Galoyan

Executive Secretary
Office of Science and Technology Policy

Subcommittee on the Social and Behavioral Sciences Team

Chair

Maya Shankar

Assistant Director for Behavioral Science
Office of Science and Technology Policy

Staff

Amira Choueiki

Executive Secretary
General Services Administration

Subcommittee Members

The following Federal departments and agencies are represented on the SBST and, through it, work together to coordinate the application of social and behavioral science research to advance policy and program goals and better serve the Nation:

- Department of Agriculture
- Department of Commerce
- Department of Defense
- Department of Education
- Department of Energy
- Department of Health and Human Services
- Department of Housing and Urban Development
- Department of Justice
- Department of Labor
- Department of Transportation
- Department of the Treasury
- Department of Veterans Affairs
- General Services Administration (Executive Secretariat)
- National Science Foundation
- Securities and Exchange Commission
- Social Security Administration
- United States Agency for International Development

The following components of the Executive Office of the President are also represented on the SBST:

- Council of Economic Advisers
- Domestic Policy Council
- National Economic Council
- Office of Management and Budget
- Office of Science and Technology Policy (Chair)

Social and Behavioral Sciences Team
Annual Report

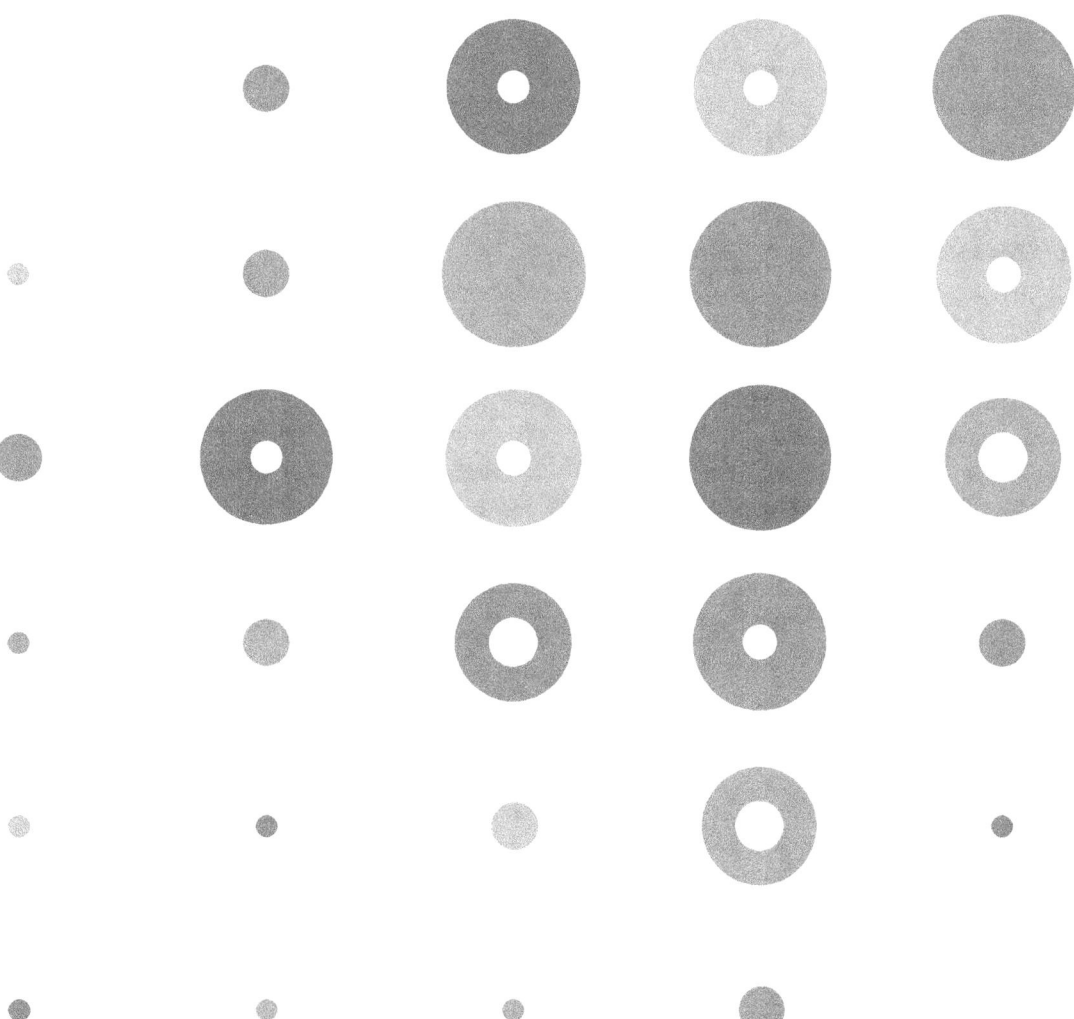

Executive Office of the President
National Science and Technology Council

September 2016

Executive Summary

On September 15, 2015, President Obama issued Executive Order 13707, "Using Behavioral Science Insights to Better Serve the American People." The Order directs Federal Government agencies to apply behavioral science insights—research insights about how people make decisions and act on them—to the design of their policies and programs.[1] The Order also charges the Social and Behavioral Sciences Team (SBST), a cross-agency group of applied behavioral scientists, program officials, and policymakers, with providing policy guidance and advice to Federal agencies in pursuit of this directive.[2]

This second annual report highlights SBST's progress in supporting the President's directive over the past year. SBST's work tracks three major themes:

- *Addressing some of the most important policy challenges facing the Nation,* such as ensuring access to affordable health insurance for the millions of Americans who still lack coverage, expanding economic opportunity for workers and their families, and reducing U.S. greenhouse gas emissions to help protect Earth's climate. SBST also applied a behavioral science perspective to the development of policy responses to the lead-contamination crisis in Flint, Michigan, and to the implementation of the recommendations of the President's Task Force on 21st Century Policing.

- *Leveraging an ever broader set of strategies to maximize impact*, from changing how programs communicate with individuals, to modifying the way programs are administered, to informing the design of policy. For example, SBST's early efforts to promote military service member enrollment in the Thrift Savings Plan (TSP), the Federal Government's workplace savings plan, began with sending informational messages to service members designed

using behavioral science insights. Since then, SBST's efforts have evolved to require that service members make choices about TSP enrollment as part of their routine orientation at pilot military bases. And most recently, SBST advised the Department of Defense on the implementation of a policy change that will automatically enroll service members into TSP starting in 2018.

- *Drawing on the best available evidence and rigorously testing the impact of its projects* to inform recommendations about what to scale and what to improve. In this spirit, SBST reports the results of all completed projects, including projects that did not yield statistically significant improvements.[3]

The report that follows presents the results of completed projects and describes ongoing efforts in eight key policy areas: promoting retirement security, advancing economic opportunity, improving college access and affordability, responding to climate change, supporting criminal justice reform, assisting job seekers, helping families get health coverage and stay healthy, and improving the effectiveness and efficiency of Federal Government operations.

The following summary highlights key efforts in each area. The results of completed projects continue to demonstrate the power of applying behavioral science insights to policy, and the works in progress provide a sense of future promise.

Promoting Retirement Security

- **Increasing retirement security for service members through automatic enrollment, active choices, and email prompts.** Enrollment in TSP by service members remains relatively low at approximately 44 percent, compared with over 87 percent for civilian Federal employees. To boost TSP participation, DOD and

---

1 Executive Order 13707 of September 15, 2015, Using Behavioral Science Insights to Better Serve the American People, *Code of Federal Regulations*, title 3 (2015): 56365–56367, https://www.gpo.gov/fdsys/pkg/FR-2015-09-18/pdf/2015-23630.pdf.

2 For more about the Social and Behavioral Sciences Team (SBST), see: https://sbst.gov.

3 Unless otherwise noted, all impact estimates reported below are statistically significant at the 5 percent level; forthcoming abstracts on https://sbst.gov also report the 95 percent confidence interval on reported impact estimates.

SBST piloted having service members make an active "Yes" or "No" choice about whether to contribute to TSP upon their arrival at a new military base, which led to an 8.3 percentage point increase in TSP enrollments. If scaled up to military bases across the country, this intervention could help promote retirement security for the service members and their families who undertake more than 640,000 transfers to new bases each year. DOD and SBST also sent emails about TSP designed using behavioral science insights to nearly 700,000 service members, which led to 4,831 new enrollments and over $1 million in additional savings in the first month of the pilot. Finally, SBST advised DOD on a policy change that will automatically enroll all new service members into TSP starting in 2018.

- **Encouraging _myRA_ enrollment for workers who lack access to workplace savings plans through timely prompts at tax time.** Roughly 68 million workers lack access to employer-sponsored retirement savings plans. In response to this need, the Department of Treasury (Treasury) created _myRA_, a starter retirement savings account. To promote enrollment, Treasury and SBST inserted prompts about _myRA_ into online tax-preparation software near the point at which filers choose how to receive their income tax refund. Preliminary findings show that highlighting the potential tax benefits of _myRA_ was a more effective tool for encouraging tax filers to open a _myRA_ account than highlighting other benefits.

- **Assisting the public with making informed decisions about when to claim Social Security retirement benefits through improved information presentation.** Social Security retirement benefits are the foundation of retirement security for tens of millions of Americans and represent 85 percent of total income on average for all lower-income individuals over 65. Individual choices—including the age at which individuals claim Social Security benefits, whether and how much to work during retirement, and how to manage claiming decisions jointly with their spouse—play an important role in how well these benefits protect against the risks of outliving one's savings. The Social Security Admin-

istration (SSA) and SBST are piloting opportunities to help the public make more informed decisions about claiming Social Security retirement benefits.

Advancing Economic Opportunity

- **Ensuring low-income children obtain, and retain, access to free or reduced-price school meals through expanded automatic enrollment and improvements to the application process.** Every year, eligible low-income students are at risk of missing out on free or reduced-price school meals offered under the National School Lunch Program (NSLP). To help ensure access to the program, the White House and the Department of Agriculture's (USDA) Food and Nutrition Service (FNS) have launched a new round of pilots that will allow states to use Medicaid data to automatically enroll students who qualify for either free or reduced-priced meals. To help eligible students retain access to school meals, FNS and SBST collaborated with over 70 school districts in the 2015–2016 school year to better communicate school-meal verification requirements to households—for example, by personalizing communications and encouraging households to take pictures of their documentation with their mobile phones for electronic submission. For the 2016–2017 school year, FNS and SBST are initiating a process change that will provide families with more time to complete their verification requirements.

- **Expanding access to credit for family farms through targeted outreach.** Since farming often produces irregular income and requires large capital investments, the USDA's Farm Service Agency (FSA) runs a program that offers small-dollar loans, known as microloans, to farmers. These loans are intended to benefit farmers who may have difficulty obtaining credit from a commercial source. To promote microloan take-up, FSA, USDA's Economic Research Service, and SBST sent outreach letters to farmers detailing customized steps for applying for a microloan and personalized contact information for their local loan officers. Letters increased the percent of farmers who obtained a microloan by 63 percent.

- **Helping student loan borrowers manage their debt by prompting the choice of more-affordable repayment plans and promoting annual recertification among those already in plans.** The Department of Education (ED) and SBST sent student loan borrowers information about income-driven repayment plans (IDR), which link monthly payments to income. A single email significantly increased IDR application rates, with more than 6,000 additional applications generated during the pilot period by borrowers with approximately $300 million in outstanding debt. To help borrowers already enrolled in IDR plans avoid monthly payment increases, ED and SBST also sent a series of messages to nearly 300,000 borrowers reminding them to recertify their IDR plans. Indicating the exact amount by which borrowers' monthly payments would increase if they did not recertify led to an 8 percent increase in recertification rates, relative to simply indicating average payment increases.

- **Encouraging borrowers in default to rehabilitate their loans by highlighting the consequences of inaction and providing borrowers with call-in times.** Each month, roughly 125,000 Federal student loan borrowers who have not made a payment in 360 days enter into default on their loans. If defaulted borrowers fail to take action, they face serious penalties including a collections fee, damage to their credit, wage garnishment, and forfeiture of Federal tax refunds. To avoid these penalties, ED offers borrowers the chance to enter into a loan-rehabilitation agreement. SBST and ED encouraged rehabilitation by sending messages to borrowers in default. Emphasizing the consequences of inaction generated 41 percent more calls to default-resolution representatives than emails emphasizing the benefits of taking action. Moreover, scheduling borrowers to call in at a specific appointment time increased the call-in rate 61 percent compared to the email emphasizing consequences of inaction.

- **Reducing the burden of student debt for individuals with disabilities through data matching and streamlined application processes.** ED offers Federal student loan relief—the Total and Permanent Disability discharge—for borrowers with certain types of disabilities. ED and SSA shared administrative data to identify around 400,000 student-loan borrowers receiving Social Security Disability Insurance who potentially qualify for a discharge of their debt. ED and SBST notified these borrowers of their potential eligibility and informed them of a streamlined version of the application form.

Responding to Climate Change

- **Supporting consumer adoption of renewable energy sources through active choices and other decision-support tools.** Adoption of green-power plans remains low at roughly 700,000 customers nationwide. SBST has initiated a dialogue with the Department of Energy's (DOE) Office of Energy Efficiency and Renewable Energy to identify the potential behavioral barriers underlying low take-up of clean energy, as well as a suite of behavioral tools that can be used to address these barriers. For example, behavioral science research indicates that prompting consumers to select a power plan from among clean and non-clean options (rather than defaulting them into a standard electricity plan) and presenting plan options in ways that facilitate informed decision-making can improve take-up. SBST will work to identify voluntary state and private-sector partners to test and evaluate these approaches on a wide scale in the coming years.

- **Improving understanding of climate change and climate patterns among non-scientists.** To help households, communities, and decision-makers better understand and adapt to the effects of rising global temperatures, SBST, the National Oceanic and Atmospheric Administration, and the University of Maryland have worked to help the United States Global Change Research Program improve their "climate indicators," which convey important information about climate patterns to non-scientists. This pilot yielded mixed results. For example, simplifying a graph showing changes in the Annual Greenhouse Gas Index increased successful interpretation of the indicator by 18 percentage points, but did not significantly increase how well people were able to draw inferences from the indicator.

Supporting Criminal Justice Reform

- **Empowering the re-entry population to thrive in their communities by developing a handbook that articulates concrete steps for individuals to take before and after their release.** To help the 40,000 inmates who are released from Federal prison each year successfully reintegrate into their communities, the Bureau of Prisons (BOP) designed a prisoner re-entry handbook. SBST contributed to the content and structure of this handbook using insights from behavioral science. For example, BOP and SBST developed checklists of action steps inmates and former inmates can take before and after their release, as well as accompanying resources to support these actions. In many cases, the timing and proper sequencing of actions are important for preventing setbacks. For example, encouraging individuals to obtain a birth certificate prior to release can accelerate their getting a government-issued photo ID and applying for work upon release. SBST also recommended that individuals be addressed as "community members" and provided ideas for how to de-stigmatize subjects such as mental health. The handbook has already been distributed to 20,000 individuals due to be released from prison.

- **Strengthening community policing and trust between law enforcement officers and the communities they serve.** The President's Task Force on 21st Century Policing published a comprehensive report in 2015 with concrete recommendations for law enforcement, local governments, community organizations, and other stakeholders. SBST distilled the report's recommendations into specific actions community members, including parents, youth, and researchers, can take. SBST is now developing

an interactive "Community Action Deck" to facilitate community-level dialogue and advocacy. The deck will articulate concrete steps communities can take toward different goals—for example, creating a community advisory board to engage law enforcement pro-actively on issues about which the community cares.

Assisting Job Seekers

- **Helping unemployed individuals return to work more quickly through changes to the way unemployment insurance benefits are administered.** The Department of Labor (DOL), the State of Oregon, and SBST are developing a pilot that would modify how unemployment insurance benefits are paid, offering workers benefits over the course of their unemployment spell that are initially higher than the standard amount, but step down over time. This pilot would build on a current Oregon-SBST pilot that is helping job seekers create and follow through on personalized work-search plans and on a Utah-SBST pilot that is waiving retrospective work-search reporting requirements in favor of submitting a prospective work-search plan. In addition, SBST and Utah have worked together to begin addressing unemployment insurance recipients as "job seekers" rather than as "claimants."

- **Facilitating the development of modern jobs and skills data platforms to effectively support labor market outcomes for workers.** DOL, the University of Chicago, and SBST are collaborating to support the *DataAtWork* project, which pools skills and jobs data, employs advanced analytical techniques to generate an understanding of what kinds of skills are being supplied and demanded, and makes the results available to workers and the organizations that support them. SBST has been conducting research to help understand labor market needs of both employers and job seekers. This research will facilitate the development of tools that can better match people to training opportunities and job openings given their unique needs and skills.

- **Supporting health insurance plan choice through streamlined plan presentation and decision-support tools.** Tens of millions of Americans now choose health insurance coverage within Federal programs that offer a selection of private plans, including the Medicare Part D prescription drug program and the Health Insurance Marketplace created by the Affordable Care Act. The Department of Health and Human Services (HHS) and SBST are working to streamline plan presentation and facilitate choices within the Federal Health Insurance Marketplace; the Center for Medicare & Medicaid Services and SBST are working to assist beneficiaries with the selection of their Medicare Part D prescription drug plan; and SBST and the Office of Personnel Management are updating the tools available to Federal employees for choosing health insurance plans in the Federal Employees Health Benefits program. In addition, SBST and HHS are designing direct outreach to the roughly 8 million families who paid a penalty for lack of coverage in 2014 to ensure they are aware of their options in future years.

- **Helping to keep families safe from the health risks when lead is found in drinking water through evidence-based communications.** As part of the Administration's response to the high levels of lead in Flint, Michigan's public water supply, the Environmental Protection Agency (EPA) and SBST designed outreach and educational materials to get clear, actionable information on reducing lead exposure and accessing free bottled water and filters into the hands of Flint residents quickly. Building on this work, SBST is exploring a broader collaboration with EPA to evaluate and improve the effectiveness of information about lead in water nationwide.

- **Minimizing the risks of foodborne illness by re-designing a food handling safety label.** Approximately 48 million cases of foodborne illness occur in the United States each year, resulting in roughly 128,000 hospitalizations and 3,000 deaths. To re-

duce foodborne hazards, the USDA's Food Safety and Inspection Service (FSIS) has developed a Safe Handling Instructions label that is required on all raw meat or poultry products. SBST is partnering with FSIS to redesign the Safe Handling Instructions label using evidence from behavioral science about the most effective ways to communicate instructions and motivate subsequent action.

- **Addressing child- and maternal-health issues world-wide through form redesign, text-message reminders, and personalized counseling.** Since 2014, USAID and SBST have been collaborating to improve child and maternal health, which has included launching and evaluating a mobile-based vaccination platform in Mozambique that allows officials to keep track of vaccine supply and remind caregivers who have missed appointments to attend upcoming ones. In 2016, selected USAID Missions joined SBST Fellows and academic experts for the first ever USAID International Behavioral Design Workshop. Projects emerging from this workshop include: increasing the number of pregnant women who receive preventive treatment for malaria by redesigning referral forms with USAID/Nigeria; increasing HIV medication adherence among high-risk populations using text-message notices and transportation subsidies with USAID/Ethiopia; and offering personalized and simplified counseling on healthy pregnancies with USAID/Nigeria and its partners.

Improving Government Effectiveness and Efficiency

- **Promoting compliant participation in refundable tax credits through timely, simplified notices.** Together with the Department of Treasury's Office of Tax Policy, tax-software developers, and academic researchers, the Internal Revenue Service (IRS) is using data-driven methods to guide its administration of refundable credits. The Earned Income Tax Credit (EITC) sent over $66 billion in income assistance to more than 27 million working families in 2015, but millions of individuals, many without children, do not claim the credit each year—either by filing a return and failing to claim the credit, or by not filing at all. One project tested the impact of mailing notices with information about tax filing and EITC participation to potentially eligible individuals who did not file a tax return in recent years. The notices resulted in a modest, but statistically significant, higher rate of tax filing, which in turn increased EITC claims. Conditional on filing, there was no significant difference in the fraction of individuals claiming the EITC, which suggests that the primary barrier to increasing EITC claims for this population is getting individuals to file a return.

- **Strengthening Federal managerial performance through a new professional-development tool.** Improving employee morale and engagement is a priority across Government. The Performance Improvement Council, DOL, DOE, and SBST developed and evaluated a new professional-development tool for Federal managers. The tool consists of an eight-module course to help managers develop eight specific traits that research shows are present in successful managers. SBST also designed a "growth mindset" intervention, which emphasized that managerial abilities are not fixed, but can be learned and strengthened over time. Research demonstrates that managers with a growth mindset are more engaged and support a culture that leads to increased worker productivity. The program concluded in early September 2016 and results will be made available soon.

Table of Contents

Introduction

On September 15, 2015, President Obama issued Executive Order 13707, "Using Behavioral Science Insights to Better Serve the American People." The Order directs Federal Government agencies to integrate behavioral science insights—research insights about how people make decisions and act on them—into the design of their policies and programs.[1] In doing so, the Order recognizes that "behavioral science insights can support a range of national priorities, including helping workers to find better jobs; enabling Americans to lead longer, healthier lives; improving access to educational opportunities and support for success in school; and accelerating the transition to a low-carbon economy."

Executive Order 13707 also charges the Social and Behavioral Sciences Team (SBST)—a cross-agency group of applied behavioral scientists, program officials, and policymakers—with providing policy guidance and advice to Federal agencies in pursuit of this directive.[2]

This second annual report highlights SBST's progress in supporting the President's directive over the past year. It builds on SBST's 2015 report, which demonstrated the value of integrating behavioral science insights into the design and administration of Government programs. As detailed in that report, SBST projects nearly doubled the rate of new enrollments in the Thrift Savings Plan (TSP) by service members, increased college enrollment among low-income students by almost nine percent, and generated more than a million dollars in Government savings, among other positive outcomes.[3]

Over the past year, SBST has focused on central policy challenges facing the Nation, such as helping millions of Americans access affordable health insurance, boosting economic opportunity for workers and families, and responding to climate change. To achieve these goals, health insurance marketplaces must be designed so that consumers can make informed decisions when selecting plans to best meet their needs, unemployment insurance programs must be structured to support job seekers and help them return to work quickly, and clean energy options must be made easy for homeowners to select from and adopt.

SBST has also brought a behavioral perspective to the Administration's response to the high levels of lead found in water in Flint, Michigan—for example, helping to ensure that families receive meaningful and up-to-date information on their water supply and evidence-based recommendations for protecting their families' health. In another effort, SBST is facilitating community-level implementation of the recommendations put forth by the President's Task Force on 21st Century Policing to promote public safety and trust.

In order to address this diverse set of challenges, SBST's approach over the past year has evolved to encompass a broader set of strategies. In addition to changing how programs communicate with individuals, SBST has also modified the way programs are administered and has informed more foundational aspects of policy design. SBST's efforts to promote retirement security among service members by encouraging TSP enrollment provide an example. This effort began with sending service members informational messages designed using behavioral insights. Since then, SBST's efforts have evolved to require that service members make choices about TSP enrollment as part of their routine orientation at pilot military bases. Most recently, SBST has been helping to inform and implement automatic enrollment in TSP for new service members, a forthcoming policy change introduced by the 2016 National Defense Authorization Act.

Finally, in the course of these efforts, SBST continues to draw on the best available evidence about what

---

1 Executive Order 13707 of September 15, 2015, Using Behavioral Science Insights to Better Serve the American People, *Code of Federal Regulations*, title 3 (2015): 56365–56367, https://www.gpo.gov/fdsys/pkg/FR-2015-09-18/pdf/2015-23630.pdf.

2 For more about the Social and Behavioral Sciences Team (SBST), see: https://sbst.gov.

3 Social and Behavioral Sciences Team, *Annual Report* (2015), https://sbst.gov/assets/files/2015-annualreport.pdf.

works and what does not. SBST also generates new evidence from its own work, designing its projects as randomized evaluations wherever possible. By doing so, SBST learns important lessons from its interventions that help inform recommendations about what to scale and what to improve. In this spirit, SBST reports the results of all of its completed projects, including projects that did not yield statistically significant improvements.[4]

_____

4 Unless otherwise noted, all impact estimates reported below are statistically significant at the 5 percent level; forthcoming abstracts on https://sbst.gov also report the 95 percent confidence interval on reported impact estimates.

The report that follows presents the results of completed projects and describes ongoing efforts in eight key policy areas: promoting retirement security, advancing economic opportunity, improving college access and affordability, responding to climate change, supporting criminal justice reform, assisting job seekers, helping families get health coverage and stay healthy, and improving the effectiveness and efficiency of Government operations. The results in this report continue to demonstrate the power of applying behavioral science insights to policy, and the works in progress provide a sense of future promise.

Behavioral Science Insights Guidance

Executive Order 13707 also calls for the Assistant to the President for Science and Technology, on behalf of SBST, to provide agencies with advice and policy guidance in pursuit of the Order. This guidance, issued alongside this report and included here as Appendix A, helps agencies identify promising opportunities to apply behavioral science insights to Federal policies and programs. It is organized around four key aspects of Federal policy where research and practice show that behavioral factors may play an especially strong role in program outcomes: determining access to programs, presenting information to the public, structuring choices within programs, and designing incentives.

Promoting Retirement Security

Retirement security in the United States is sometimes said to rest on a three-legged stool, comprising workplace pensions, private savings, and Social Security retirement benefits.[5] Federal policies support each component by incentivizing employers to offer retirement savings vehicles and contribute on behalf of their employees, encouraging private retirement savings, and providing Social Security benefits.

Behavioral science insights have already informed retirement policy in important ways. For example, the Pension Protection Act of 2006, which facilitated the practice of automatically enrolling workers into employer-sponsored workplace savings plans, is based on research showing that switching from an opt-in to an opt-out enrollment system dramatically increases participation rates.[6] Since the implementation of this policy, automatically enrolling workers into 401k plans and automatically escalating their contribution rates over time have led, by some estimates, to billions of dollars in additional savings by Americans.[7]

Working in this tradition, SBST is using behavioral science insights to encourage Federal workers to participate in workplace savings plans and to assist them with contribution decisions and portfolio choices; to help individuals build their private savings with new offerings such as *my*RA; and to enable workers to get the most out of their Social Security retirement benefits.

Workplace Savings Plans

Plan Participation

Since 2010, civilian agencies have automatically enrolled new hires in the Thrift Savings Plan (TSP), the Federal Government's defined contribution plan, and enrollment rates for civilian Federal employees are relatively high at 87 percent. Military employees at the Department of Defense (DOD), by contrast, are not currently automatically enrolled, and participation rates are correspondingly lower at 44 percent.[8]

In 2015, Congress passed and President Obama signed the 2016 National Defense Authorization Act (NDAA) which, in combination with other reforms to military retirement, mandates automatic enrollment for new military service members into TSP starting in 2018.[9] Beginning at that time, TSP accounts will automatically be opened for the more than 100,000 service members who join the military each year, and DOD will make contributions equal to 1 percent of basic pay and matching contributions up to 5 percent.[10] SBST is advising DOD on this policy change and is helping to implement key aspects—for example, determining when and how service members will be presented with the opportunity to opt out, and designing tools that will assist service members in making investment decisions and changes to contribution rates.

Automatic enrollment into TSP will help service members who join the military after 2017 build a secure retirement, but other solutions are needed for incumbent service members who will not be affected by this policy change. One 2015 SBST pilot demonstrated that sending a one-time email promoting TSP enrollment to the more than 800,000 non-enrolled service members nearly doubled the rate of new TSP enrollments.[11]

The pilot resulted in approximately 5,000 new enrollments and over $1 million in additional savings in just

---

5 See e.g.: https://www.ssa.gov/history/stool.html.

6 Pension Protection Act of 2006, Public Law 109-280, U.S. Statutes at Large 120 (2006): 780–1172; Brigitte C. Madrian and Dennis F. Shea, "The Power of Suggestion: Inertia in 401(k) Participation and Savings Behavior," *Quarterly Journal of Economics* 116 (2001): 1149–1187.

7 Shlomo Benartzi and Richard H. Thaler, "Behavioral Economics and the Retirement Savings Crisis," *Science* 339 (2013): 1152–1153.

8 For general background information on TSP, see: www.tsp.gov. Enrollment rates for TSP as of late 2014 are reported here: www.frtib.gov/pdf/minutes/MM-2014Dec-Att1.pdf. The differing enrollment procedures are described at: tsp.gov/planparticipation/eligibility/establishingAccount.html.

9 National Defense Authorization Act for Fiscal Year 2016, Public Law 114-92, U.S. Statutes at Large 129 (2015): 726–1309.

10 See: http://www.defense.gov/News/Article/Article/612742/dod-announces-recruiting-retention-numbers-through-june-2015.

11 Social and Behavioral Sciences Team, *Annual Report* (2015), 30.

one month. A second 2015 SBST pilot demonstrated that prompting service members to make an optional decision about TSP when they were transferring to a new military base increased TSP enrollment rates by roughly 4.3 percentage points.[12]

In 2016, SBST and DOD expanded on this prior work by implementing an "active choice" intervention at two military bases. Behavioral science research shows that requiring employees to choose whether or not to enroll in a workplace savings plan is an effective tool for boosting savings plan enrollment.[13] Compared with SBST's 2015 study which prompted an optional choice, this intervention required service members to make a decision about TSP enrollment as they were transferring to new military bases.[14]

SBST and DOD implemented the pilots at Army installations in Ft. Bragg, North Carolina and Ft. Lewis, Washington. At Ft. Bragg, service members were required to submit a modified TSP Election Form with three options: "Yes, I choose to enroll and save," "No, I choose not to enroll and save," or "I'm already enrolled." The modified portion of the form is shown in Figure 1. At Ft. Lewis, service members were asked to raise their hand at orientation if they wanted to enroll in TSP, and

were then led to computers to enroll online. Service members were also provided with a cover sheet and video highlighting the benefits of TSP saving.

As shown in Figure 2, requiring an active choice resulted in substantially higher TSP enrollment rates. Enrollment rates at Ft. Bragg and Ft. Lewis during the five-week pilot period were 10.7 percent and 8.4 percent, respectively, compared to a maximum of 1.9 percent at the other three bases. Taking into account differences across both the time periods and the different bases, the active choice intervention led to an estimated 8.3 percentage point increase in the probability of a service member enrolling in TSP within 4 weeks of the orientation.

Contribution Rates

Increasing participation in defined contribution plans is essential for retirement security, but it is far from sufficient. Workers also need to make decisions and take actions to fund their accounts at adequate levels. In one pilot, DOD and SBST tested the impact of promoting TSP enrollment and highlighting specific TSP contribution rates in an email message.[15] Nearly 700,000 non-enrolled service members were each sent: an email with no mention of a contribution rate, one of eight emails highlighting a contribution rate between 1 and 8 percent, or no email at all.

12 Social and Behavioral Sciences Team, *Annual Report* (2015), 31.

13 Gabriel D. Carroll, James J. Choi, David Laibson, Brigitte C. Madrian, and Andrew Metrick, "Optimal Defaults and Active Decisions," *Quarterly Journal of Economics* 124 (2009): 1639–1674.

14 Further details on this and other reported projects are forthcoming on https://sbst.gov.

15 James J. Choi, Emily Haisley, Jennifer Kurkoski, and Cade Massey, "Small Cues Change Savings Choices," (NBER Working Paper No. 17843, 2012).

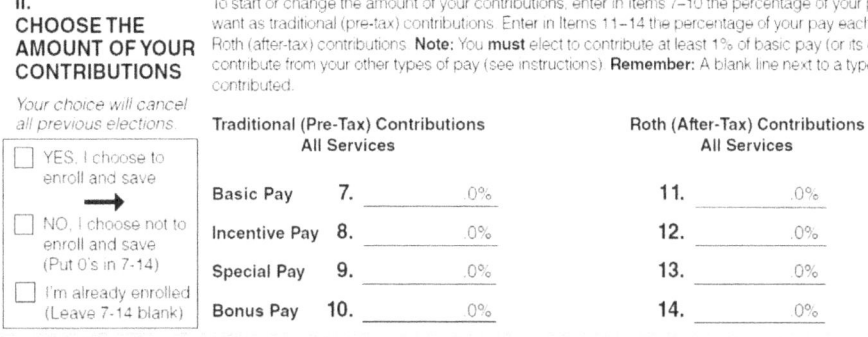

Figure 1: TSP Active Choice

Notes: As part of an active choice pilot, service members at Fort Bragg were required to submit a modified TSP election form that included the box at the left asking them to indicate their choice among the three options.

Figure 3 shows the fraction of each group that signed up for TSP in February 2016. Service members who were sent the emails that incorporated behavioral science insights had an average enrollment rate that was 0.7 percentage point higher than those who had not been sent an email. Enrollment rates varied with suggested contribution rates, with the highest enrollment rate (3.0 percent) observed for service members who received the email highlighting the lowest contribution rate, of 1 percent. Suggesting specific contribution rates also significantly increased the likelihood that service members signed up for TSP at that contribution rate. For example, those service members sent an email suggesting a 7 percent contribution rate were more likely to enroll at exactly 7 percent than those who did not receive an email suggesting that contribution rate.

Overall, the email communications increased enrollment in TSP—4,831 more service members enrolled as a result of being sent a message designed using behavioral insights, representing over $1 million in new contributions. While enrollment rates were slightly higher when suggested contribution rates were 1 or 2 percent, there were no significant differences in enrollment rates across the emails that suggested rates between 3 and 8 percent. This indicates that higher suggested contribution rates between 3 and 8 percent do not substantially depress enrollment rates for these individuals.

Portfolio Choice

In addition to choosing how much to contribute to retirement accounts, plan participants must also choose how to invest within those accounts. Portfolio allocations should match individuals' preferences, plans for retirement, and risk tolerance. SBST, Treasury, and the Office of Personnel Management (OPM) are collaborating on a research project to analyze and understand trends in enrollment, contribution rates, and fund election among new civilian Federal employees who are automatically enrolled into TSP. Beginning in 2010, new civilian employees were automatically enrolled at a 3 percent contribution rate, with 100 percent of contributions allocated to the TSP's G Fund (a fund invested in short-term U.S. Treasury securities specially

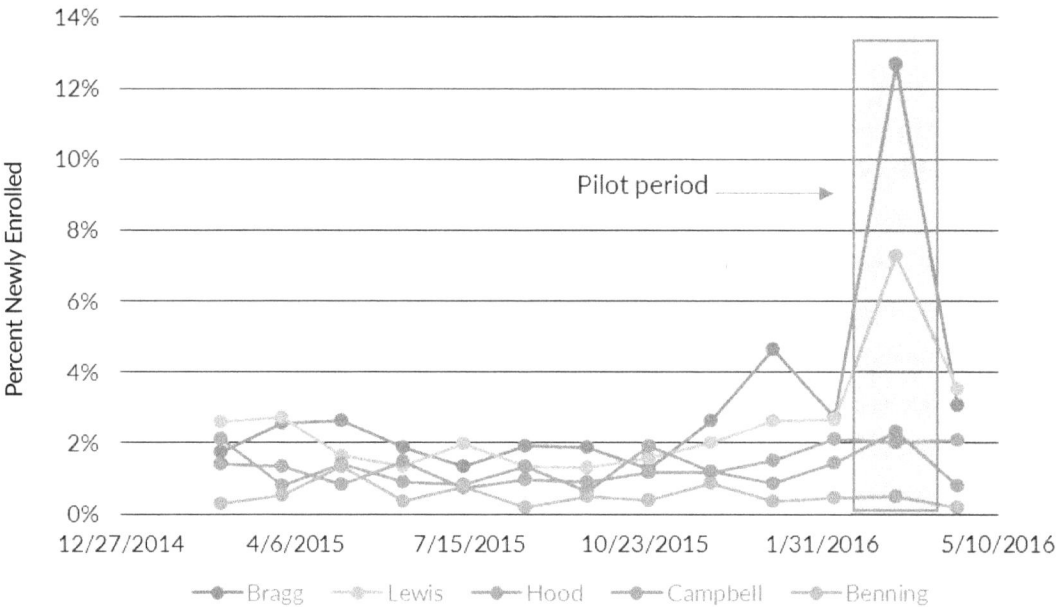

Figure 2: TSP Enrollment Rates at Pilot and Comparison Bases Prior to, During, and After the Active Choice Pilot Period

Notes: Enrollment rates for TSP among non-enrolled, in-processing service members at the pilot bases and comparison bases during the pilot period and the pre- and post- periods. Bragg and Lewis are the pilot bases; Hood, Campbell, and Benning are the comparison bases.

issued to the TSP).[16] The G Fund is a safe investment, but for many employees, it may be overly conservative. In 2015, TSP changed its default allocation to a lifecycle fund, an L Fund, that invests in a mix of assets tailored to meet the objectives of a target retirement date (e.g., 2050).[17] Data on portfolio allocations of employees with start dates before and after this policy change will provide evidence on the degree to which individuals stick with their default option and will inform future outreach to employees about the benefits of an L Fund.

Private Savings

Approximately 68 million workers do not have access to a retirement savings plan at work and must therefore save in other ways.[18] To help address this issue, the Administration has proposed automatically enrolling workers who lack access to a workplace savings plan into Individual Retirement Accounts (IRAs). The Department of Labor has issued guidance and proposed rules that allow states to implement similar arrangements.[19]

In addition, Treasury has created a starter retirement savings account called *my*RA. *my*RA has no fees, no minimum contributions, and carries the same tax advantages as a Roth IRA. Moreover, *my*RA investments are backed by the U.S. Treasury and safely earn interest. Individuals can set up a *my*RA online at *my*RA.gov and fund their account via payroll direct deposit, one-time or recurring deposits from checking or savings accounts, or at tax time by directing portions of their tax refund to their *my*RA.

16 Office of Personnel Management, *Federal Employee Participation Patterns in the Thrift Savings Plan* 2008–2012, (June 2015).

17 See: https://www.tsp.gov/InvestmentFunds/FundOptions/index.html.

18 https://www.whitehouse.gov/blog/2016/06/02/states-taking-action-boost-worker-retirement-savings.

19 The proposal for automatic enrollment in IRAs is described here: www.whitehouse.gov/sites/default/files/omb/budget/fy2017/assets/opportunity.pdf.
The proposed DOL rule is available here: https://www.federalregister.gov/articles/2015/11/18/2015-29426/savings-arrangements-established-by-states-for-non-governmental-employees.

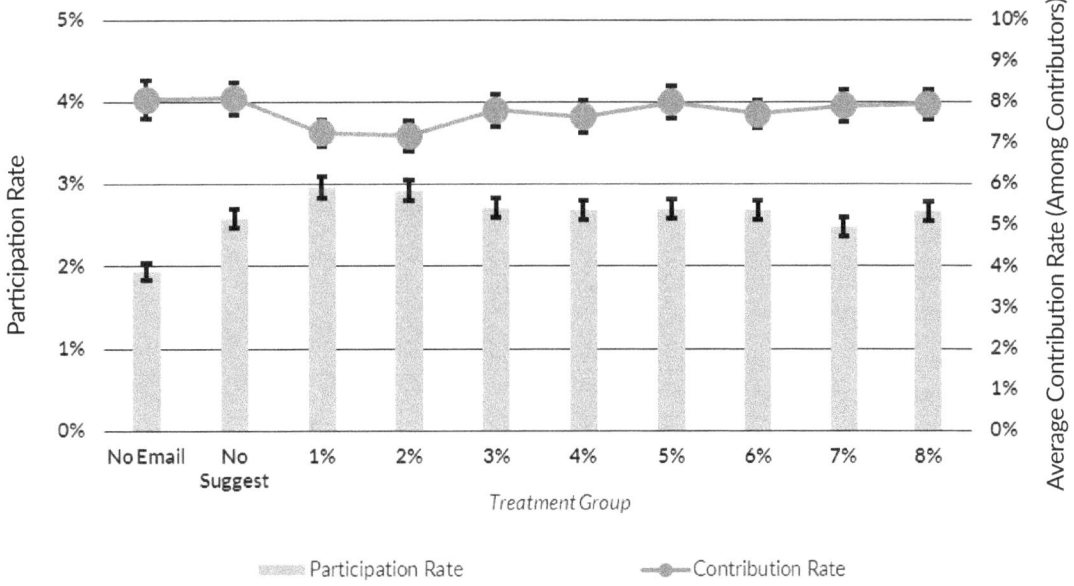

Figure 3: TSP Participation and Contribution Rates in February 2016 by Suggested Contribution Rate

Notes: Percentage of service members enrolling in TSP in February 2016 by suggested contribution rate. Error bars display 95 percent confidence intervals. n = 699,674.

Treasury, with input from SBST and other experts in behavioral science, developed and piloted a number of messages designed to introduce *my*RA to tax filers over the past year. The messages prompted filers to learn more and, if interested, open a *my*RA and potentially contribute some of their tax refund to their *my*RA. The pilot leveraged behavioral science research showing that tax time, when most filers receive a refund, can be an effective moment for encouraging savings.[20] Messages were inserted either in online tax-preparation software near the point at which tax filers choose how to receive their tax refund or in pre-tax season communications.

Preliminary findings from this pilot suggest that highlighting the potential tax benefits of *my*RA may be more effective at encouraging tax filers to learn about and open a *my*RA than highlighting other benefits. Additional findings and analysis from this effort will be available in late 2016 and will inform future Treasury outreach.

Social Security

Social Security is the foundation of retirement security for tens of millions of Americans. Social Security represents about 85 percent of all income for lower-income individuals over 65.[21] Individual choices—including the age at which individuals claim Social Security benefits, whether and how much to work in retirement, and how to manage claiming decisions jointly with one's spouse—play an important role in how well these benefits protect against the risks of outliving one's savings. Research in behavioral science sheds light on how people make these kinds of choices, which can in turn inform program design and administration.[22]

In one pilot currently in development, SSA and SBST are focusing on people's decision to work while claiming retirement benefits. Before full retirement age, monthly benefits are subject to a retirement earnings test (RET) which reduces monthly benefits by fifty cents for every dollar that individuals earn above an exempt amount ($15,720 in 2016). This reduction in benefits is offset by an increase in monthly benefits once workers reach their full retirement age. That is, the RET defers rather than reduces benefits.[23] If workers incorrectly perceive the RET to be a permanent reduction in benefits, they may make decisions about working and claiming benefits based on imperfect information.[24] SSA and SBST are developing a pilot project to test alternative ways of communicating about the RET in order to help workers make informed decisions about how much to work and when to claim benefits.

20 Michal Grinstein-Weiss, Blair D. Russell, William G. Gale, Clinton Key, and Dan Ariely, "Behavioral Interventions to Increase Tax-Time Saving: Evidence from a National Randomized Trial," *Journal of Consumer Affairs* (2016).

21 James M. Poterba, "Retirement Security in an Aging Population," *American Economic Review* 104 (2014): 1–30.

22 Melissa Knoll, "The Role of Behavioral Economics and Behavioral Decision Making in Americans' Retirement Savings Decisions," *Social Security Bulletin* 70 (2010): 1–23.

23 Social Security Administration, *How Work Affects Your Benefits*, (2014).

24 Jeffrey B. Liebman and Erzo F. P. Luttmer, "Would People Behave Differently If They Better Understood Social Security? Evidence from a Field Experiment," *American Economic Journal: Economic Policy* 7 (2015): 275–299; Jeffrey R. Brown, Arie Kapteyn, Olivia S. Mitchell, and Teryn Mattox, "Framing the Social Security Earnings Test," (Pension Research Council working paper WP2013-06, 2013).

Advancing Economic Opportunity

The Federal Government supports economic opportunity through numerous programs, from nutrition assistance for school children to programs that support the growth of small businesses and family farms.

These programs are most effective at promoting economic opportunity when they are designed from a behavioral perspective, reflecting the needs and realities of those they intend to serve. Behavioral science research shows, for example, that seemingly small barriers to program access—such as complex information, burdensome applications, or poorly presented options—can potentially decrease take-up and participation by eligible individuals.[25]

Over the past year, SBST has worked to expand access to nutrition assistance programs, boost the effectiveness of income support programs, and help small businesses grow.

Nutrition Assistance

The National School Lunch Program (NSLP) provides meals to more than 30 million children nationwide.[26] Ensuring that all eligible children from low-income households have access to free or reduced-price school meals is an important policy objective, and behavioral science research suggests that automating enrollment can be among the most effective tools for promoting program participation. Two recent policy changes reflect movement in this direction: The 2004 Child Nutrition and WIC Reauthorization Act requires schools to automatically qualify students from households that receive Supplemental Nutrition Assistance Program (SNAP) for free meals.[27] And the Healthy,

Hunger-Free Kids Act of 2010 creates the Community Eligibility Provision, which allows high-poverty schools to provide free meals to all of their students without the need for individual students or their families to file applications.[28]

Building on the Administration's multi-year efforts to streamline access to school meals, the White House and the Department of Agriculture's Food and Nutrition Service (FNS) have launched a new round of pilots that will allow states to use Medicaid data to automatically enroll students into NSLP for free or reduced-priced meal benefits. Eleven states currently use Medicaid data to directly certify students for NSLP, and FNS aims to expand this approach to 20 total states over the next 3 years.[29] These pilots will further reduce the need for school-meal household applications among students whose program eligibility can be established using Medicaid data and will increase program integrity.

SBST has also taken a number of additional steps to streamline access to NSLP for low-income students who will not benefit from direct certification and must still submit applications. For example, SBST, FNS, and the Presidential Innovation Fellows are creating a web-based application that school districts can adapt for their own use to simplify complex instructions and enable households to sign up easily for NSLP using their mobile phones.

While boosting enrollment into NSLP is an important part of the solution to food insecurity, each year eligible students lose access to these benefits by failing to complete verification requirements. Therefore, it is equally important to help currently enrolled, eligible students maintain their participation in the program. Research indicates that in past years as many as half

---

25 Marianne Bertrand, Sendhil Mullainathan, and Eldar Shafir, "Behavioral Economics and Marketing in Aid of Decision Making Among the Poor," *Journal of Public Policy & Marketing* 25 (2006): 8–23; Anuj K. Shah, Sendhil Mullainathan, and Eldar Shafir, "Some Consequences of Having Too Little," Science, 338 (2012): 682–685.

26 See: http://www.fns.usda.gov/sites/default/files/NSLPFactSheet.pdf.

27 Child Nutrition and WIC Reauthorization Act of 2004, Public Law 108-265, U.S. Statutes at Large 118 (2015): 729–790.

28 For more information on CEP, see: http://www.fns.usda.gov/school-meals/community-eligibility-provision.

29 http://www.fns.usda.gov/request-applications-participate-new-demonstrations-evaluate-direct-certification-medicaid.

There are 3 ways to submit the following documents for [Mary Jones, Tom Jones, and Steven Jones] **by** [Oct 16]:

📱 Take pictures of the requested documents with your phone/camera and email them to [e-mail]. **Include a picture of this page.**

OR

✉ Mail copies of the documents (or originals) **along with this page** [to mailing address] using the pre-paid envelope provided. Originals will be sent back.

OR

▦ Come in person to the office located at [address] to drop off the documents. **Please bring this page with you.**

Questions? Contact [Juanita Price] at [the toll free number] [(xxx)-xxx-xxxx] or at [e-mail address].

Figure 4: Detail of the Redesigned NSLP Verification Letter

Notes: Detail of the redesigned verification letter highlighting the ability of recipients to use their mobile phone to photograph and email required documentation.

of students who lost access to school meals for failing to submit verification paperwork were, in fact, eligible for free or reduced-price meals.[30]

To help address this issue, FNS and SBST have launched a multi-year effort to streamline the process of NSLP verification. In the first phase, implemented in school year 2015–2016, SBST worked with over 70 school districts to better communicate verification requirements to households using behavioral science insights. SBST redesigned communications to include personalized information; distill a complicated set of instructions into three easy steps; and encourage households to take pictures of their documentation with their mobile phones and electronically submit them to schools, rather than sending in paper copies.[31] In the second phase, SBST and FNS are partnering with school districts around the country to initiate a process change in the 2016–2017 school year that will give families more time to submit their verification information.

Income Support

The Federal Government offers income support to low-income individuals and families through a variety of programs and tax credits. For example, the Supplemental Security Income (SSI) program, administered by the Social Security Administration (SSA), provides an important source of income security to aged, blind, and disabled individuals with low income and assets. Participation in SSI among qualified individuals is estimated to be around 50 percent.[32] Low participation rates persist among the elderly even as they benefit from relaxed eligibility rules (e.g., disability is not a requirement to receive SSI after 65, as it is at earlier ages).[33] Newly eligible 65-year-olds may therefore be unaware, at least initially, of their eligibility. SSA and SBST are developing a notice targeted to individuals who have recently turned 65 and appear, based on information available in SSA records, to be eligible for SSI.

SSI requires that participants report changes in their earnings to SSA because eligibility and payment amounts are determined, in part, by income levels.[34]

---

30 A 2004 USDA case study found that many of the households that failed to respond to LEA verification requests were, in fact, income eligible for the benefits that were awarded to them at the time their applications were processed. See Report No. CN-04-AV3 at http://www.fns.usda.gov/sites/default/files/NSLPcasestudy.pdf.

31 Philip James Edwards, Ian Roberts, Mike J. Clarke, Carolyn DiGuiseppi, Reinhard Wentz, Irene Kwan, Rachel Cooper, Lambert M Felix, Sarah Pratap, "Methods to Increase Response to Postal and Electronic Questionnaires," *The Cochrane Library* (2009); Benjamin L. Castleman and Lindsay C. Page, "Summer Nudging: Can Personalized Text Messages and Peer Mentor Outreach Increase College Going Among Low-Income High School Graduates?," *Journal of Economic Behavior & Organization* 115 (2015): 144–160.

32 Kathleen McGarry and Robert F. Schoeni, "Understanding Participation in SSI," (University of Michigan Retirement Research Center (MRRC) Working Paper, WP 2015-319, 2015).

33 Kathleen McGarry, "Factors Determining Participation of the Elderly in Supplemental Security Income," *Journal of Human Resources* 31 (1996): 331–358.

34 SSI reporting responsibilities are summarized here: https://www.ssa.gov/ssi/text-report-ussi.htm.

In 2015, SSA partnered with SBST and researchers from academia to promote program compliance in SSI. SSA tested the impact of sending different messages encouraging wage reporting to 40,000 SSI recipients. Preliminary results show that these messages led to a small increase (0.3 percentage point) in the likelihood that SSI recipients reported countable earnings in the five months following the pilot, a 28 percent increase over the baseline probability of reporting earnings in the control group. Variations in messaging did not have a significant impact on reporting. Data collection on this project will continue in order to determine whether and when these letters have an effect on other outcomes, such as program savings and work efforts. A final report on the project is expected in 2017.

Small Business

Federal policies also support small businesses, such as family farms, through credit programs and by providing business development resources. For example, because farming often produces irregular income and requires large capital investments, USDA runs a program that offers small-dollar loans, known as microloans, to in-need farmers. These loans are intended to benefit farmers who may have difficulty obtaining credit from a commercial source. To help meet the financing needs of small, beginning, and non-traditional farm operations, USDA's Farm Service Agency (FSA), USDA's Economic Research Service (ERS), and SBST designed an outreach letter that provided farmers across the country with information on the benefits of the microloan program, as well as personalized contact information for local loan officers. This project builds on earlier SBST efforts that led to small but significant increases in microloan uptake.[35] Farmers who were sent this letter were 22 percent more likely to apply for and receive a loan.

In addition to microloans, FSA runs a suite of other programs to support farmers and ranchers, in areas including disaster relief and conservation. FSA operations are overseen at the local level by an elected County Committee (COC). Participation in COC elections has declined over time, endangering the model

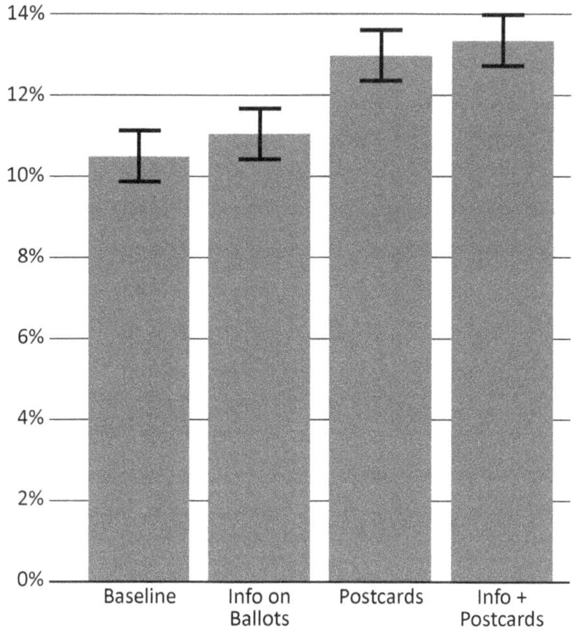

Figure 5: Turnout Rates in County Elections by Treatment Group

Notes: Turnout rates in 2015 FSA COC elections by treatment group. Error bars display 95 percent confidence intervals. n = 1,399,307

of local representation that the Committees provide. In an effort to increase voter turnout, FSA partnered with ERS and SBST to test changes to COC election ballots and outreach material.

For COC elections, voters receive and return ballots by mail. SBST implemented two changes to FSA voter outreach mailings: candidate information was printed on the outside of ballot, and postcards with candidate information were sent to voters to first remind them of the upcoming election and then again to remind them of the ballot submission deadline. Eligible voters were randomly assigned to be sent one of the following: traditional ballots, ballots with candidate information, traditional ballots and postcards, or ballots with candidate information and postcards. As shown in Figure 5, among those sent ballots with candidate information and postcards, voter turnout was 12.2 percent, a 2.9 percentage point increase in turnout relative to those receiving traditional ballots. Given a postcard cost of approximately $0.05 per unit, the cost of encouraging each additional voter to cast a ballot was $1.72.

35 Social and Behavioral Sciences Team, *Annual Report*, (2015), 37.

To support other small businesses, the Small Business Administration (SBA) provides resources that teach essential skills. The online SBA Learning Center hosts 58 courses on a variety of topics—including "Contracting Opportunities for Veterans," "Financing Options for Small Businesses," and "How to Write a Business Plan"—and receives over 20,000 visitors per month. To encourage greater utilization of these resources, SBA and SBST streamlined the online registration procedure by reordering and reducing the amount of requested information. These changes reduced the time required to complete the form, but still collected the information essential to SBA. During the three months that the new forms were piloted, 64.0 percent of us-

ers continued on to the course, compared with 57.7 percent in the three months before the changes were implemented, an increase of 6.3 percentage points.

And finally, SBST is making it easier for entrepreneurs and young and small businesses to promote and protect their businesses. Recent research suggests that delays in patent application approvals may be especially costly for small firms.[36] SBST is working with the U.S. Patent and Trademark Office to streamline the trademark application for applicants who are not using the services of a lawyer.

36 Joan Farre-Mensa, Deepak Hegde, and Alexander Ljungqvist, "The Bright Side of Patents," (NBER Working Paper No. 21959, 2016).

Behavioral Interventions to Advance Self-Sufficiency

SBST's work to apply behavioral science to a wide range of Federal programs builds on pioneering efforts by the Administration for Children and Families (ACF) in the U.S. Department of Health and Human Services. The Behavioral Interventions to Advance Self-Sufficiency (BIAS) project launched in 2010 and has been sponsored by ACF's Office of Planning, Research, and Evaluation and led by MDRC. The BIAS project completed 15 experiments (with nearly 100,000 sample members) in the areas of child support, child care, and work support. In 11 of the 15 randomized controlled trials, behavioral "nudges" like reminders or simplified, personalized letters had a statistically significant impact on at least one primary outcome.[37]

ACF is continuing this work with a new set of tests.[38] In addition, ACF's Office of Child Support Enforcement (OCSE) has awarded funds to explore behavioral interventions specific to the area of child support.[39] SBST has partnered with OCSE to engage with state and local child support agencies that received this funding as they develop initial intervention ideas.

ects can be found here: http://www.acf.hhs.gov/programs/opre/research/project/behavioral-interventions-to-advance-self-sufficiency.

38 Information on the BIAS next generation project can be found here: http://www.acf.hhs.gov/programs/opre/behavioral-interventions-to-advance-self-sufficiency-bias-next-generation-2015-2022.

39 Information on the BICS (Behavioral Interventions for Child Support Services) project can be found here: http://www.acf.hhs.gov/media/press/2014/acf-grant-to-explore-link-between-psychology-behavior-and-child-support-payments.

37 The BIAS project concludes in 2016, and the final report is forthcoming. Previously released reports on individual proj-

Improving College Access and Affordability

Having a college education has never been more important for the economic success of Americans.[40] Federal policies and programs, such as Federal financial aid, help make higher education more accessible for students and their families. At the same time, rising student loan debt presents a challenge for many borrowers. The Federal Government offers loan borrowers the choice of different repayment plans, including income-driven repayment plans (IDR) which link student loan payments to borrowers' monthly incomes, to help them manage their payments.

Insights from behavioral science have already had an impact on the design and operation of Federal financial aid. In response to research showing that the lengthy and complex Free Application for Federal Student Aid (FAFSA) delayed or deterred some students from going to college, the Department of Education (ED) took a series of steps to streamline the FAFSA—for example, allowing applicants to skip questions that do not pertain to them and enabling applicants to automatically fill parts of the application using information from their tax return.[41] Moreover, in previous work with SBST, ED boosted IDR enrollment rates using low-cost behavioral strategies.[42]

Building on this work, SBST has continued to collaborate with ED and with other Federal agencies to help unlock college access for more students and to help borrowers more effectively manage their student loan debt.

College Access

To promote college access, the Administration has undertaken extensive efforts to promote FAFSA awareness and completion—for example, making the application available earlier in the school year so that more students can use expected levels of financial support to inform their decisions about whether and where to apply to college, which may in turn support college access.[43] Contributing to these efforts, SBST has engaged in a series of pilot projects to help promote access to financial aid and increase college enrollment.

For example, the Department of Housing and Urban Development (HUD) interacts with a large population of students who may benefit from increased and early knowledge about Federal financial aid. To take advantage of this opportunity for direct outreach, SBST collaborated with HUD and ED on a project to increase FAFSA completion and college enrollment among HUD-assisted families.

In March 2016, HUD sent nine variations of mailers to a total of 45,000 youth and full-time students living in subsidized housing. Mailers were sent to coincide with tax season, when families were likely to have the necessary financial information available to complete the FAFSA. Mailers had different combinations of messengers and formats. The pilot design also included a control group that did not receive a mailing. Preliminary results show that individuals sent a mailing completed the FAFSA at a slightly higher rate than the control group (22.3 percent versus 22.0 percent), but the difference was not significant. Differences across letter variations were not statistically significant.

For students already in college, maintaining their access to financial aid can be an important source of financial and educational stability. Students must renew their FAFSA annually in order to maintain their financial aid, but many do not. In recent years, 15 to 20 percent of freshman Pell Grant recipients in good academic standing have failed to successfully

40 Claudia Dale Goldin and Lawrence F. Katz, *The Race between Education and Technology*, (Harvard University Press, 2009).

41 Eric P. Bettinger, Bridget Terry Long, Philip Oreopoulos, and Lisa Sanbonmatsu, "The Role of Application Assistance and Information in College Decisions: Results from the H&R Block FAFSA Experiment," *Quarterly Journal of Economics* 127 (2012): 1205–1242. U.S. Department of Education, "Fiscal Year 2017 Budget: Summary and Background Information," (2016), p. 46.

42 Social and Behavioral Sciences Team, *Annual Report*, (2015), 35

43 See a description of this change the FAFSA application timeline at: https://studentaid.ed.gov/sa/about/announcements/fafsa-changes

re-file their FAFSA.[44] Based on behavioral science research showing that communications to students in school can effectively address this issue, ED and SBST conducted an email campaign in July 2015 targeting freshman borrowers who were at risk of not continuing their academic program.[45] Using data from the National Student Loan Data System, ED identified and sent emails to approximately 195,000 freshman borrowers who were enrolled in May 2015, had not yet renewed their FAFSA, and, based on ED models, were at risk of leaving school. The emails reminded borrowers that they should either renew their FAFSA or prepare for loan repayment if they were not planning to return to school. Data will be collected through January of 2017 at which point a full analysis will be completed.

Affordable Loan Repayment

Over 41 million student loan borrowers carry a total of more than $1.26 trillion dollars in outstanding Federal student loan debt.[46] IDR plans can help Americans manage this debt by limiting their monthly payments to a percentage of their discretionary income and providing for potential loan forgiveness. Despite recent increases in the number of IDR enrollments, fewer than 15 percent of borrowers are enrolled in IDR.[47]

ED introduced the Revised Pay As You Earn (REPAYE) IDR plan in December 2015 to simplify and expand IDR eligibility. To promote access to REPAYE and other IDR plans, ED and SBST collaborated on a large-scale email campaign that notified over 3 million borrowers about the availability and benefits of such plans. This work built on earlier trials by ED and SBST that successfully increased IDR application rates.[48]

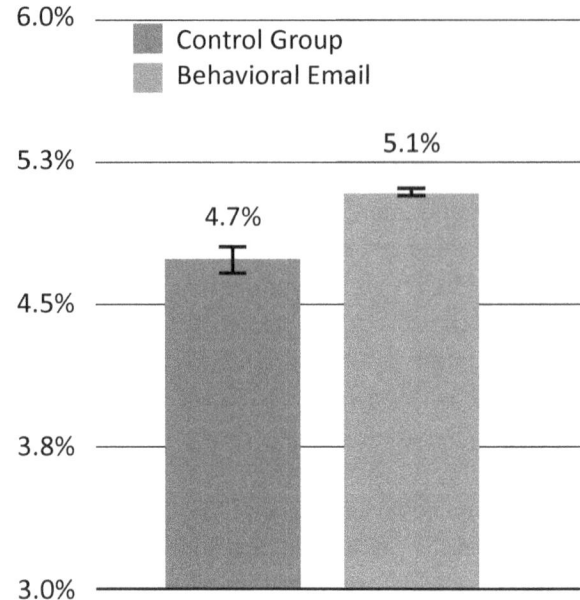

Figure 6: IDR Submission Rates after Email

Notes: Percentage of individuals submitting an IDR application by July 2016. n = 3,036,691.

The email campaign tested the effectiveness of sending emails in general and also of tailoring email content to borrowers' circumstances. The campaign sent emails to four groups of borrowers not already in an IDR plan: borrowers who indicated interest in IDR either from a previous application or during loan counseling; borrowers in economic forbearance or deferment; borrowers in delinquency; and borrowers with Federal Family Education Loans (FFEL) who needed to consolidate loans before entering an IDR plan.

The email tailored to those who had expressed interest in IDR emphasized action and decreased recipient uncertainty by stating "You are guaranteed to qualify." The email was also personalized, noting that the recipient had "shown interest" in IDR.[49] The email designed for those in forbearance and deferment used a loss frame and highlighted how bor-

44 Kelli Bird and Benjamin L. Castleman, "Here Today, Gone Tomorrow? Investigating Rates and Patterns of Financial Aid Renewal Among College Freshmen," EdPolicyWorks working paper (2014).

45 Benjamin L. Castleman and Lindsay C. Page. "Freshman Year Financial Aid Nudges: An Experiment to Increase FAFSA Renewal and College Persistence," *Journal of Human Resources* 51 (2016): 389-415.

46 Federal Student Aid, Annual Report FY 2016, (2016); data available at: https://studentaid.ed.gov/sa/about/data-center/student/portfolio

47 Ibid.

48 Social and Behavioral Sciences Team, *Annual Report* (2015), 35.

49 Philip James Edwards, Ian Roberts, Mike J. Clarke, Carolyn DiGuiseppi, Reinhard Wentz, Irene Kwan, Rachel Cooper, Lambert M. Felix, and Sarah Pratap, "Methods to Increase Response to Postal and Electronic Questionnaires," *The Cochrane Database of Systematic Reviews* 3 (2009): Art. No.: MR000008.

rowers' monthly payments could remain at $0.[50] The email to delinquent borrowers prompted them to either "Act Now" to sign up for IDR or "Do Nothing" and potentially face negative impacts to their credit rating.[51] These targeted emails were tested against two generic emails sent to all groups.

Overall, emails were an effective means for prompting IDR enrollment. Figure 6 compares application rates between those who were sent an email and those in the control group. Sending emails increased IDR applications by 0.4 percentage point over the control submission rate of 4.7 percent over a three month time frame. This means that a single email led approximately 6,000 more borrowers, with approximately $300 million in outstanding debt, to sign up for IDR.

The effectiveness of targeting messages to each group was less clear. The targeted email was most effective for borrowers in deferment; but different messages' effects could not be distinguished from one another in the other borrower cohorts. SBST and ED will continue to examine the benefits of tailoring messages based on the characteristics of recipients.

In order for individuals to continue in an IDR plan, they must complete an annual recertification process to update their income and family size. More than half of borrowers fail to recertify their IDR plan each year, which means their payments revert to what they would be under the standard 10-year repayment plan, which are typically higher.[52]

Between June and October 2015, ED and SBST sent emails to borrowers who were nearing their IDR recertification dates and would see an increase in their monthly payments if they failed to recertify their plans. In one pilot, 140,000 borrowers were sent either a ge-

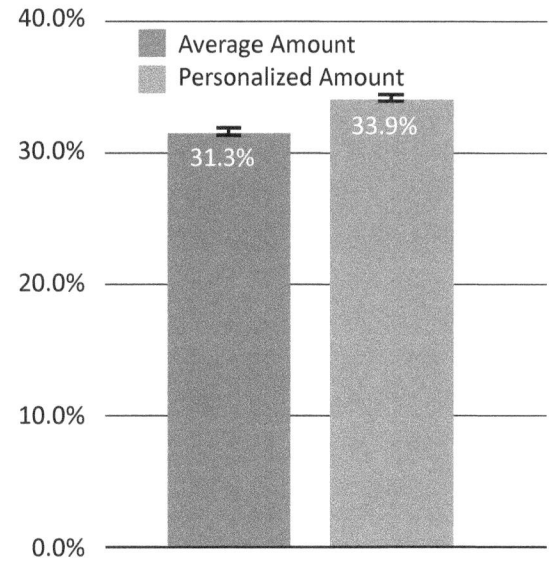

Figure 7: IDR Recertification Rates

Notes: Percentage of individuals recertifying their IDR plan in June 2015. n = 142,505.

neric email stating the average payment increase seen across IDR borrowers, or a personalized email indicating the specific amount that their payment would increase. As shown in Figure 7, the personalized email led 33.9 percent of borrowers to recertify, a 2.6 percentage point increase over the generic email. A separate pilot prompting IDR recertification sent 100,000 borrowers a set of three reminder emails, but varied the timing of the reminders. One group was sent reminders spaced 31 days apart and a second group was sent reminders delivered on consecutive days (the day before, the day of, and the day after their recertification deadline). Recertification rates were indistinguishable between the two groups.

Some borrowers who have difficulty making payments end up defaulting on their student loans. Each month, roughly 125,000 Federal student loan borrowers who have not made a payment in 360 days enter into default.[53] If borrowers fail to act in the following 60 days, their loans are transferred to a private

---

50 Daniel Kahneman and Amos Tversky, "Prospect Theory: An Analysis of Decision Under Risk," *Econometrica* 47 (1979): 263–291.

51 Eleanor Putnam-Farr and Jason Riis, "'Yes, I want to enroll.': Yes/No Response Formats Increase Response Rates in Marketing Communications," (working paper, 2015).

52 Katy Hopkins and Karen McCarthy, "ED Unveils New Pilot Programs On Recertification Notifications For Certain Borrowers In Income-Driven Repayment Plans," National Association of Student Financial Aid Administrators (2015). http://www.nasfaa.org/news-item/631.

53 Monthly average over the period April 2015 through May 2016 based on the Department of Education Debt Management and Collections System data. Note that due to seasonal variation, the number of borrowers included in the monthly study cohorts is fewer than the average.

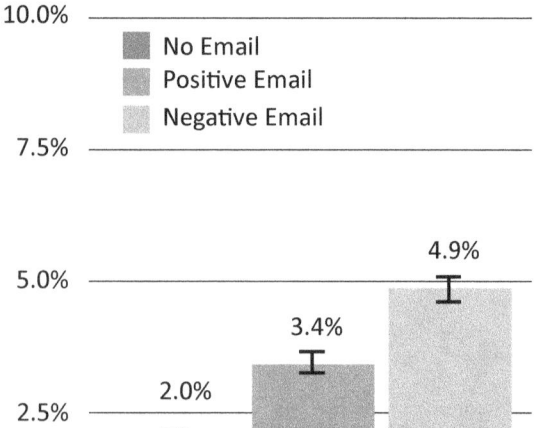

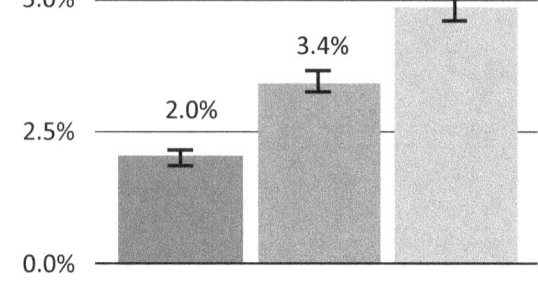

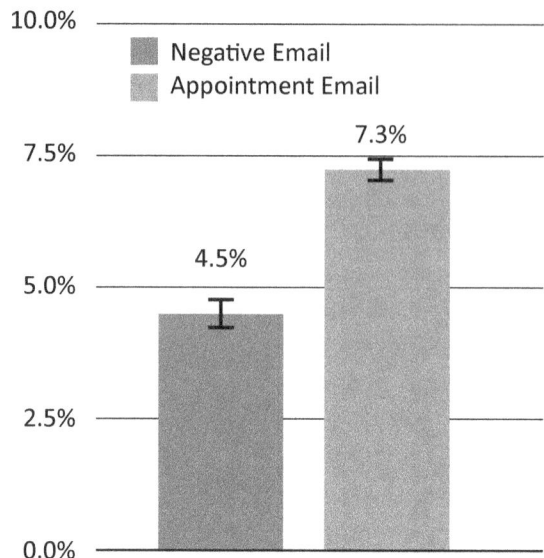

Figure 8: Defaulted Borrower Call-In Rates in Spring 2015

Notes: Percentage of defaulted borrowers calling in regarding their loan in spring 2015. n = 66,182.

Figure 9: Defaulted Borrower Call-In Rates in July 2015

Notes: Percentage of defaulted borrowers calling in regarding their loan in July 2015. n = 65,403.

collections agency and they face penalties, damage to their credit, wage garnishment, ineligibility for future Federal student aid, and forfeiture of IRS tax refunds. To avoid these penalties, ED offers borrowers the chance to enter into a loan rehabilitation agreement that allows them to exit default if they make nine out of ten payments, typically at reduced levels.

ED and SBST conducted a series of iterative pilots from April through July 2015, prompting borrowers in default to contact ED to enter a rehabilitation agreement. While longer-term data collection is needed to determine the impact of these messages on rates of successful loan rehabilitation, there were two intermediate findings of interest. Messages emphasizing the negative consequences of inaction were more effective at generating calls to default resolution representatives than were more positive messages emphasizing the benefits of rehabilitation.[54] Figure 8 displays this result, showing that negative emails led to a 1.4 percentage point increase in the call-in rate compared with positive emails.

The second finding is that when an additional 65,000 borrowers were sent either the negatively framed email or an email with similar messaging that also contained a specific appointment time during which to call, the email with the suggested call-in time further increased call rates by 2.8 percentage points.[55] See Figure 9.

Finally, ED offers loan relief for borrowers with certain types of disabilities, known as the Total and Permanent Disability (TPD) discharge. These borrowers are eligible to have their Federal student loan obligations discharged, meaning the remaining balance on the student's loan would be forgiven.[56] In order to ensure that qualifying individuals are aware of this program and to streamline the application process, in 2016 ED and the Social Security Administration (SSA) identified around 400,000 individuals who have student loan balances, are currently receiving Social Security Disability Insurance (SSDI), and may qualify for a discharge. In addition, by virtue of being identified as receiving SSDI,

54 Daniel Kahneman and Amos Tversky, "Prospect Theory: An Analysis of Decision Under Risk," *Econometrica* 47 (1979): 263–291.

55 Social and Behavioral Sciences Team, *Annual Report* (2015), 42.

56 For more information on Total and Permanent Disability (TPD) discharge process, see: https://www.disabilitydischarge.com.

these individuals are able to complete an abbreviated version of the application. ED worked with SBST on the design and content of letters to these individuals, informing them of the option to have their loans discharged and the steps required to do so. The initial letter outreach was completed in August 2016.

Early Childhood Education

During the first three years of life, children from low-income families hear millions fewer total words than their peers in more affluent families.[57] This deficit, known as the word gap, is associated with disparities in vocabulary development and critically, in school readiness.[58] Social science has shed light on one low-cost solution: providing parents with behavioral reminders, feedback, and resources on how to improve the frequency and quality of interactions with their babies can significantly improve the number of positive, engaging verbal exchanges that babies experience.

To put these research insights into practice, the state of Georgia, through a public-private partnership of six organizations, has launched Talk With Me Baby (TWMB).[59] TWMB is a multi-sector, interdisciplinary initiative committed to ensuring that every newborn in Georgia receives essential "Language Nutrition"—language sufficiently rich in engagement, quality, quantity, and context that it nourishes the child neurologically, socially, and linguistically. To date, TWMB has trained more than 1,000 WIC staff, and over 350 pediatric, Ob/Gyn, hospital, and public health nurses and medical professionals in Language Nutrition coaching for new parents. For example, the neonatal intensive care unit (NICU) at Children's Healthcare of Atlanta at Egleston, part of Georgia's largest regional perinatal center, has responded to research showing the positive impact that abundant Language Nutrition can have on preterm babies by requiring that all NICU staff be trained as "Language Nutrition coaches."

TWMB is leveraging tablets and similar technology to disseminate trainings so that the instruction can be tailored to meet the diverse learning needs of providers and caregivers, allow for sustained two-way interactions between the provider and caregiver population, and provide for real-time assessments of TWMB implementation and outcomes.

Leaders in other states across the country have taken note of TWMB and have shown interest in replicating the TWMB model. In response, with technical support from OSTP, and in partnership with the Barbara Bush Foundation for Family Literacy, TWMB developed an online toolkit to bring this model to scale. The toolkit makes all of TWMB's curricula, training tools, and marketing and promotional assets readily accessible. A coalition of groups in seven other states (Arizona, Arkansas, Connecticut, Florida, Mississippi, Rhode Island, and Utah) has already committed to utilizing this toolkit to integrate the concepts of TWMB in workforces already reaching parents and babies, as a part of a long-term effort to help all children achieve the critical milestone of reading proficiency by the end of third grade.

---

57 Betty Hart and Todd R. Risley, *Meaningful Differences in the Everyday Experience of Young American Children*, (Baltimore, MD: Brookes, 1995).

58 Jeanne Brooks-Gunn, Cecilia E. Rouse, and Sara McLanahan, "Racial and Ethnic Gaps in School Readiness," in *School Readiness and the Transition to Kindergarten in the Era of Accountability*, ed. R.C. Pianta, M.J. Cox, and K.L. Snow, 283–306 (Baltimore, MD: Brookes, 2007).

59 See: https://www.whitehouse.gov/blog/2014/12/12/talk-me-baby-increasing-early-learning-opportunities-every-child-georgia.

Responding to Climate Change

There is no greater challenge facing the Nation and the world than climate change. The Federal Government works to protect the environment, expand the clean energy economy, and prepare communities for the effects of climate change. To accomplish these goals, the Government performs many functions, including regulating power plants, encouraging the development and utilization of clean sources of energy, and collecting and disseminating information to consumers, communities, and decision makers.[60]

Behavioral insights have already been used to inform energy policy in a number of different contexts.[61] For example, research shows that individuals reduce their residential energy consumption when provided with information about how their consumption compares with that of their neighbors.[62] In another example, rates of clean-power adoption were dramatically higher in Germany when consumers had to opt out of clean energy plans rather than opt in.[63]

SBST is working to reduce carbon emissions and conserve energy by promoting clean-power adoption and helping homeowners make homes more energy efficient. SBST is also testing ways to better communicate information about climate change and climate patterns to non-scientists.

Renewable Energy and Energy Efficiency

Addressing climate change requires developing and utilizing renewable sources of energy, such as wind and solar power. The availability of renewable energy

offerings for consumers is expanding—in 2015, wind and solar combined outpaced natural gas in new electricity-generation capacity added to the grid.[64] Reflecting these trends, many residential electricity consumers now have the option to source their power from clean energy resources. Consumers can purchase clean energy directly from their utility's clean-power program or from electricity suppliers that support the expansion of renewable-energy demand. Adoption of clean-power plans, however, remains low at approximately 700,000 customers nationwide. [65]

The market mechanisms by which clean-power plans induce, or fail to induce, additional supply of clean energy is debated in the literature.[66] Perhaps less appreciated are the behavioral factors that might affect the performance of these markets—for example, lack of awareness of clean-power options, barriers to enrollment such as needing to connect current utility accounts to a third-party account,[67] and difficulty choosing from a vast array of options.[68] Behavioral science provides tools for addressing some of these challenges, such as automatic enrollment and active choices, as the Germany opt-out example illustrates.[69] Provid-

60 See: https://www.whitehouse.gov/the-record/climate.

61 Hunt Allcott and Sendhil Mullainathan, "Behavior and Energy Policy," *Science* 327 (2010): 1204–1205.

62 Hunt Allcott, "Social Norms and Energy Conservation," *Journal of Public Economics* 95 (2011): 1082–1095; Hunt Allcott and Todd Rogers, "The Short-Run and Long-Run Effects of Behavioral Interventions: Experimental Evidence from Energy Conservation," *American Economic Review* 104 (2014): 3003–3037.

63 Felix Ebeling and Sebastian Lotz, "Domestic Uptake of Green Energy Promoted by Opt-Out Tariffs," *Nature Climate Change* 5 (2015), 868–871; Daniel Pichert and Konstantinos V. Katsikopoulos, "Green Defaults: Information Presentation and Pro-Environmental Behaviour," *Journal of Environmental Psychology* 28 (2008): 63–73.

64 Energy Information Administration (EIA) calculations from the Preliminary Monthly Electric Generator Inventory, data available at http://www.eia.gov/electricity/data/eia860m/. For a summary of these calculations, see: http://www.eia.gov/todayinenergy/detail.cfm?id=25492.

65 Jenny Heeter, *Status and Trends in the U.S. Voluntary Green Power Market (2013 Data)*, (National Renewable Energy Laboratory Technical Report, 2014).

66 e.g. see Michael Gillenwater, Xi Lu, Miriam Fischlein, "Additionality of Wind Energy Investments in the U.S. Voluntary Green Power Market," *Renewable Energy* 63 (2014): 452–457.

67 In competitive markets it is possible for users to switch to a different utility that might offer green power. In other markets, purchasing green power is only possible through an arrangement with a single utility that will continue to provide power, but may obtain power from a particular source if demanded by the consumer.

68 Cass R. Sunstein and Lucia A. Reisch, "Behaviorally Green: Why, Which and When Defaults Can Help," in *New Perspectives for Environmental Policies Through Behavioral Economics*, eds. F. Beckenboch and W. Kahlenborn, 161–194 (Springer International, 2016).

69 Felix Ebeling and Sebastian Lotz, "Domestic Uptake of Green Energy Promoted by Opt-Out Tariffs," *Nature Climate Change* 5 (2015), 868–871; Daniel Pichert and Konstantinos V. Katsikopoulos, "Green Defaults: Information Presentation and Pro-Environmental Behaviour," *Journal of Environmental Psychology* 28 (2008): 63–73.

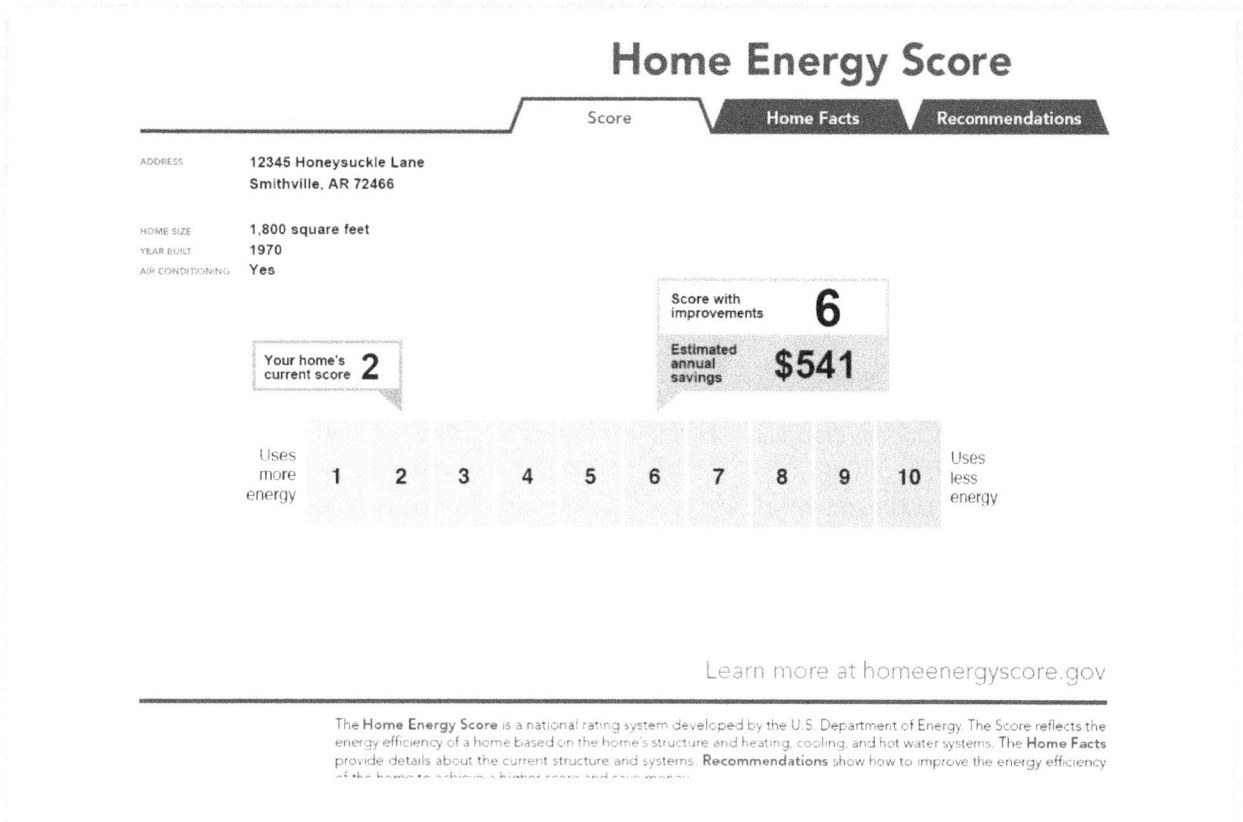

Figure 10: Example of a Home Energy Score Report

Notes: An example of the summary portion of a Home Energy Score Report.

ing clear information about the costs and benefits of clean energy may also encourage customers to sign up for clean-energy purchases.[70]

SBST has initiated a dialogue with the Department of Energy's (DOE) Office of Energy Efficiency and Renewable Energy to identify the potential behavioral barriers underlying low take-up of clean energy, as well as a suite of behavioral tools that can be used to address these barriers. For example, behavioral science research indicates that prompting consumers to select a power plan from among clean and standard options (rather than defaulting them into a standard electricity plan) may help increase participation rates.[71] SBST will identify vol-

untary state and private-sector partners to test and evaluate these approaches on a wide scale over the next few years.

In other work with DOE, SBST is contributing to the design and evaluation of the Home Energy Score, a DOE program that provides homeowners and potential home buyers with verified information to quickly assess the energy-efficiency profile of a home (see Figure 10).[72] The Home Energy Score also provides homeowners with clear recommendations for improving the energy efficiency of their home. Results of the project are expected in 2017.

---

70 Dorian Litvine and Rolf Wüstenhagen, "Helping 'Light Green' Consumers Walk the Talk: Results of a Behavioural Intervention Survey in the Swiss Electricity Market," *Ecological Economics* 70 (2011): 462–474.

71 Gabriel D. Carroll, James J. Choi, David Laibson, Brigitte C. Madri-

an, and Andrew Metrick, "Optimal Defaults and Active Decisions," Quarterly Journal of Economics 124 (2009): 1639-1674.

72 For more on Home Energy Score, see: http://energy.gov/eere/buildings/home-energy-score. In addition, the U.S. EPA, through the ENERGY STAR program, also offers a variety behavior-based solutions to help consumers reduce the greenhouse emissions that cause climate change. See: www.energystar.gov.

Information and Adaptation

SBST's other climate-related efforts focus on adaptation—that is, responding to and managing the effects of rising global temperatures. For example, the United States Global Change Research Program (USGCRP) is compiling indicators that can be used to track ecological, biological, and social impacts of climate change.[73] SBST, researchers at the National Oceanic and Atmospheric Administration (NOAA), and academic researchers at the University of Maryland have collaborated to help USGCRP develop climate indicators that reflect research about how to effectively communicate information to non-scientists.

This project gauged comprehension of 14 existing USGCRP indicators using an online survey that asked people between three and six questions about the information presented in each indicator. The two indicators with the lowest proportion of correct responses—the Annual Greenhouse Gas Index and Annual Heating and Cooling Degree Days—were re-

designed. Figure 11 shows how the Greenhouse Gas indicator (a measure of the capacity of the Earth's atmosphere to trap heat due to long-lived greenhouse gasses) was simplified by removing a second y-axis and reordering and relabeling the legend to improve clarity.

A second online survey measured comprehension of the redesigned versions. Results suggest that simple design changes hold promise for improving comprehension of climate information. The redesigned versions resulted in a greater proportion of correct responses to some comprehension questions, but not others. For example, changes to the Annual Greenhouse Gas Index indicator increased correct responses to questions that assessed how well people understand the information presented in the indicator by 18 percentage points (from 57 percent to 75 percent), but did not significantly increase how well people were able to draw inferences from the indicator. Results for the other redesigned indicator—Annual Heating and Cooling Degree Days—were similarly mixed.

73 See: http://www.globalchange.gov/explore/indicators

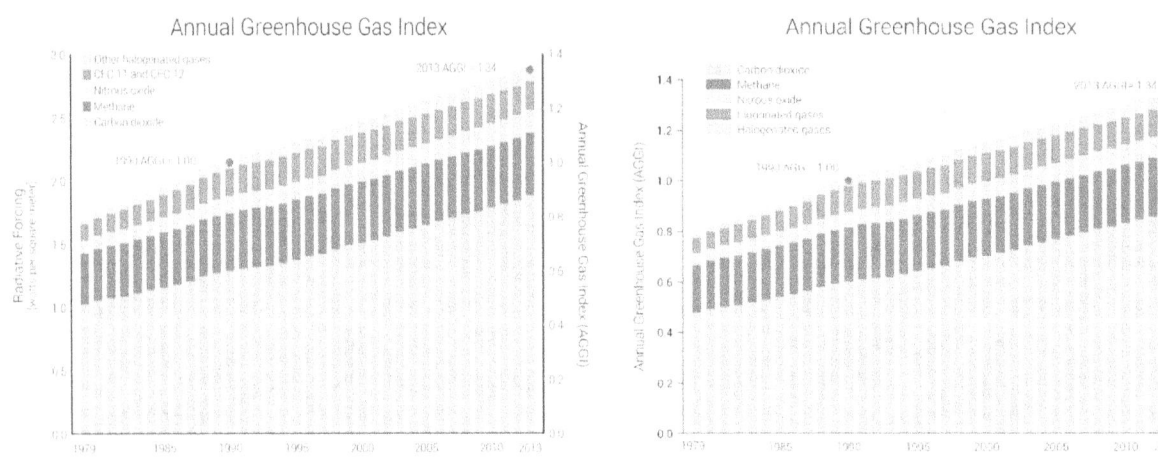

Figure 11: Example of a Redesigned Climate Indicator

Notes: This figure displays the original visualization of the indicator on the left, compared with a redesigned version on the right.

Supporting Criminal Justice Reform

The Administration has taken critical steps to reform the criminal justice system, including establishing the Task Force on 21st Century Policing, the Police Data Initiative, and the Data-Driven Justice Initiative. These initiatives have advanced concrete strategies for communities seeking to build trust and to enhance relationships between local law enforcement and the communities they serve. These efforts have also focused on removing unnecessary barriers that may prevent formerly-incarcerated individuals from pursuing educational and employment opportunities.

Insights from behavioral science can play an important role in criminal justice reform.[74] For example, applying behavioral science insights to programs that support juvenile offenders led to a significant reduction in readmission rates to a juvenile detention center.[75] Over the past year, SBST addressed two criminal justice issues at the Federal level: supporting the re-entry of formerly incarcerated individuals into their communities and encouraging community involvement in policing reform.

Prisoner Re-Entry

The Bureau of Prisons (BOP) releases more than 40,000 Federal inmates each year.[76] Research indicates that presenting individuals with customized services and a strategy for re-entry (e.g., concrete steps for how to obtain a driver's license, health insurance, shelter, transportation, employment, and healthcare) leads to significantly lower arrest

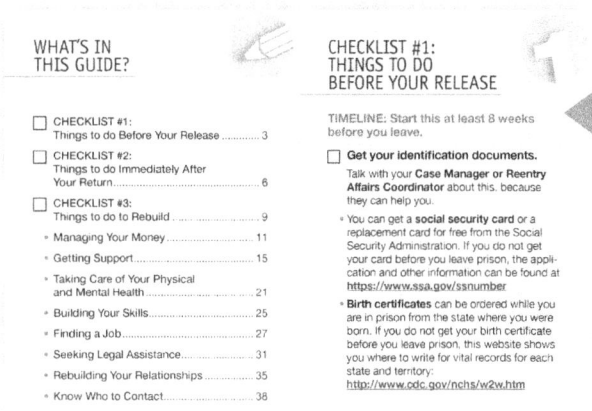

Figure 12: Bureau of Prisons Re-Entry Handbook

Notes: Example of checklist from re-entry handbook.

rates following release.[77] This year, BOP designed a re-entry handbook to assist individuals with their transition. SBST contributed to the content and structure of the handbook using insights from behavioral science. For example, BOP and SBST developed three checklists of discrete steps to take at three different points in time: immediately before release, within one week of returning home, and within one month of returning home (see Figure 12).[78] In many cases, the proper timing and sequencing of steps is important for preventing setbacks. For example, encouraging individuals to obtain a birth certificate and any education records prior to release can accelerate their ability to obtain a government-issued photo ID and apply for work upon release.

---

74 See, for example, Part 3 of the following volume: Eldar Shafir, ed., *The Behavioral Foundations of Public Policy*, (Princeton, 2012), which reviews behavioral science insights with relevance for the justice system.

75 Sara B. Heller, Anuj K. Shah, Jonathan Guryan, Jens Ludwig, Sendhil Mullainathan, Harold A. Pollack, "Thinking, Fast and Slow? Some Field Experiments to Reduce Crime and Dropout in Chicago," (NBER Working Paper No. 21178, 2015).

76 Yearly release number reports can be retrieved here: https://www.bop.gov/about/statistics/statistics_inmate_releases.jsp.

77 Anthony A. Braga, Anne M. Piehl, and David Hureau, "Controlling Violent Offenders Released to the Community: An Evaluation of the Boston Reentry Initiative," *Journal of Research in Crime and Delinquency* 46 (2009): 411–436; Philip J. Cook, Songman Kang, Anthony A. Braga, Jens Ludwig, and Mallory E. O'Brien, "An Experimental Evaluation of a Comprehensive Employment-Oriented Prisoner Re-Entry Program," *Journal of Quantitative Criminology* 31 (2015): 355–382.

78 Available here: https://www.bop.gov/resources/pdfs/reentry_handbook.pdf.

The handbook also provides advice and resources on longer-term actions, such as how to manage one's finances and continue one's education. SBST reviewed each recommendation to ensure it was broken down into discrete steps and connected individuals to relevant resources, such as organizations that help people navigate housing and legal services. SBST also recommended that individuals be addressed as "community members" and provided ideas for how to de-stigmatize subjects such as mental health.[79] The handbook has so far been distributed to 20,000 individuals due to be released from prison.

Community Involvement in Policing Reform

In December 2014, President Obama signed an Executive Order creating the Task Force on 21st Century Policing to build trust between law enforcement officers and the communities they serve.[80] The Task Force published a comprehensive report in 2015 with concrete recommendations for law enforcement, local governments, community organizations, and other stakeholders.[81] SBST synthesized the report's recommendations into specific actions community members, including parents, youth, and researchers, can take. SBST is now developing an interactive "Community Action Deck" to facilitate community-level dialogues.[82] Each card in the deck will articulate concrete steps communities can take toward different goals. For example, one card will outline steps for creating a community advisory board to engage law enforcement proactively on issues of interest in the community. Each card will include an example of one community that has successfully implemented that action.

79 Marilynn B. Brewer and Wendi Gardner, "Who is this "we"? Levels of Collective Identity and Self Representation," *Journal of Personality and Social Psychology* 71 (1996): 83–93; Yan Chen and Li Sherry Xin, "Group Identity and Social Preferences," *American Economic Review* 99 (2009): 431–457.

80 Executive Order 13684 of December 18, 2014, Establishment of the President's Task Force on 21st Century Policing, *Code of Federal Regulations,* title 3 (2014): 76865–76866, https://www.gpo.gov/fdsys/pkg/FR-2014-12-23/pdf/2014-30195.pdf.

81 President's Task Force on 21st Century Policing, *Final Report of the President's Task Force on 21st Century Policing*, (Washington, DC: Office of Community Oriented Policing Services, 2015), http://www.cops.usdoj.gov/pdf/taskforce/taskforce_finalreport.pdf.

82 Todd Rogers, Katherine L. Milkman, Leslie K. John, and Michael I. Norton, "Beyond Good Intentions: Prompting People to Make Plans Improves Follow-Through on Important Tasks," *Behavioral Science & Policy* 1 (2015).

Assisting Job Seekers

Good jobs are the cornerstone of economic stability for most Americans, and well-functioning labor markets are essential for the health of the overall U.S. economy. A number of Federal policies support job search, employment, and skill development through job search assistance, job training programs, the provision of labor market information, and unemployment insurance (UI).

Research from behavioral science magnifies and deepens our understanding of the ways in which individual well-being depends on meaningful employment, showing how unemployment can cause not only financial, but also psychological and physical duress.[83] By accounting for core features of human psychology, behavioral science also sheds light on solutions that help people return to work and improve labor market outcomes.[84] For example, research finds that a UI system which frontloads benefit payments to the beginning of a UI spell, rather than evenly distributing payments over time, may help people return to work more quickly.[85]

SBST has been working over the past year to help job seekers find employment more quickly, to better match the skills of individuals with the demands of employers by developing and sharing higher quality information about labor markets, and to improve access to job training opportunities.

Job Search and Employment

The Federal-state UI program provides a source of income security to those who lose employment through no fault of their own, and provided 6.5 million job seekers with a total of $32 billion of benefits in 2015.[86] At the same time, by design UI strives to help job seekers return to work quickly.[87] Behavioral science insights, by providing a more complete understanding of how individuals experience and respond to spells of unemployment, can inform how to pay out UI benefits and design supporting UI activities to assist workers and help speed their return to work.[88] Drawing on this research, SBST is collaborating with several state agencies to implement and evaluate UI program changes.

The Department of Labor (DOL), the State of Oregon's UI agency (Oregon), and SBST are working to pilot one set of these changes to UI policy design and implementation. SBST, DOL, and Oregon are discussing a potential pilot that would modify how UI benefits are paid over the course of their unemployment spell, offering workers benefits that are initially higher than the standard amount but step down over time. That is, while the total amount of the benefit would remain roughly the same, on average, benefits would be front-loaded to the beginning of a period of unemployment. As noted above, behavioral science research shows that this kind of payment structure may help people return to work more quickly. [89]

This project would build on an SBST pilot with the Oregon Employment Department (OED) that is currently ongoing in seven WorkSource Oregon (WSO) field of-

83 David J. Roelfs, Eran Shor, Karina W. Davidson, and Joseph E. Schwartz, "Losing Life and Livelihood: A Systematic Review and Meta-Analysis of Unemployment and All-Cause Mortality," *Social Science & Medicine* 72 (2011): 840–854; Karsten I. Paul and Klaus Moser, "Unemployment Impairs Mental Health: Meta-Analyses," *Journal of Vocational Behavior* 74 (2009): 264–282.

84 Linda Babcock, William J. Congdon, Lawrence F Katz, and Sendhil Mullainathan, "Notes on Behavioral Economics and Labor Market Policy, IZA *Journal of Labor Policy* 1 (2012): 1–14.

85 Stefano DellaVigna, Attila Lindner, Balázs Reizer, Johannes F. Schmieder, "Reference-Dependent Job Search: Evidence from Hungary," (NBER Working Paper No. 22257, May 2016).

86 U.S. Department of Labor Employment & Training Administration, "Unemployment Insurance Data Dashboard," retrieved July 15, 2016 from: http://oui.doleta.gov/unemploy/DataDashboard.asp.

87 Martin N. Baily, "Some Aspects of Optimal Unemployment Insurance," *Journal of Public Economics* 10 (1978): 379–402; Raj Chetty, "Moral Hazard vs. Liquidity in Optimal Unemployment Insurance," *Journal of Political Economy* 116 (2008):173–234.

88 Stefano DellaVigna and M. Daniele Paserman, "Job Search and Impatience," *Journal of Labor Economics* 23 (2005): 527–588; Johannes Spinnewijn, "Unemployed but Optimistic: Optimal Insurance Design with Biased Beliefs," *Journal of the European Economic Association* 13 (2015): 130–167.

89 Stefano DellaVigna, Attila Lindner, Balázs Reizer, Johannes F. Schmieder, "Reference-Dependent Job Search: Evidence from Hungary," (NBER Working Paper No. 22257, May 2016); Steven Shavell and Laurence Weiss, "The Optimal Payment of Unemployment Insurance Benefits over Time," *Journal of Political Economy* (1979): 1347–1362.

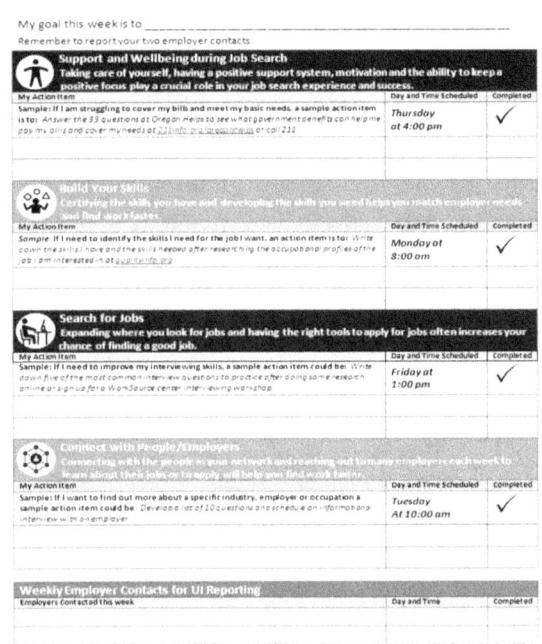

Figure 13: The Oregon Personal Employment Plan

Notes: Detail of the Oregon Personal Employment Plan.

---

fices, and which helps job seekers create and follow through on proactive work-search plans. The pilot requires individuals to create a forward-looking, 4-week long employment plan during their first in-person meeting with WSO staff. The employment plan template, a portion of which is shown in Figure 13, breaks out work-search activities into four categories: support and well-being, skill building, job search, and connecting with people and employers.[90] Job seekers are prompted to indicate a completion date for each action item, which research shows can increase the likelihood of following through.[91] In addition to the plan, job seekers also receive a letter and biweekly emails reminding them about their plans and available resources.[92] At the end of the 4 weeks covered by

the plan, job seekers are emailed and encouraged to create a voluntary, updated plan. Results showing the impacts of the employment plan on job search activities, patterns of UI claims, and employment and wage outcomes are expected in September 2017.

In another collaboration, SBST is supporting the Utah Department of Workforce Services (DWS) with the design and evaluation of changes to aspects of the Utah UI program. For example, based on research finding that individuals sometimes may take different actions depending on which aspects of their self-identity are more salient, Utah has updated some official UI communications to address recipients as "job seekers" rather than as "claimants."[93]

Utah and SBST are also testing the feasibility and impact of changes to the work-search requirements that individuals face while on UI. Workers claiming UI benefits in Utah are required to report four new job contacts they made in the prior week. In 2015, DWS implemented a pilot that offered randomly-selected job seekers the option of creating a six-week, forward-looking employment plan in lieu of their regular, retrospective reporting requirements.

The goal of the small-scale pilot (recruiting was conducted until 50 claimants opted in) was primarily to gauge operational feasibility, as well as the attractiveness of the employment plan option among claimants. DWS found that few job seekers took the option of completing the employment plan instead of traditional reporting. DWS is currently using the lessons from the first phase to field a second phase pilot in which a revised, three-week employment plan is presented as the default reporting requirement for a selected group of job seekers. The second phase pilot began in July 2016, with results expected in 2017.

Many other Federal programs, in addition to UI, attempt to balance providing support for individuals

90 Jeroen J. G. van Merrienboer and John Sweller, "Cognitive Load Theory and Complex Learning: Recent Developments and Future Directions," *Educational Psychology Review* 17 (2005): 147–177.

91 Peter M. Gollwitzer and Paschal Sheeran, "Implementation Intentions and Goal Achievement: A Meta-Analysis of Effects and Processes," *Advances in Experimental Social Psychology* 38 (2006): 69–119.

92 Madhu Sudan Mohanty, "Effects of Positive Attitude and Optimism on Employment: Evidence from the US Data," *Journal of Socio-Economics* 39 (2010): 258–270.

93 George A. Akerlof and Rachel E. Kranton, "Economics and Identity," *Quarterly journal of Economics* (2000): 715–753; Robyn A. LeBoeuf, Eldar Shafir, and Julia Belyavsky Bayuk, "The Conflicting Choices of Alternating Selves," *Organizational Behavior and Human Decision Processes* 111 (2010): 48–61.

with providing assistance and resources for returning to work. Disability insurance (DI) both provides for those unable to work and supports self-sufficiency. In ongoing work with the Social Security Administration (SSA) and the Office of Management and Budget (OMB), SBST helped design new outreach to disability insurance applicants who were determined to be ineligible for the program. SSA mailed letters to roughly 40,000 denied applicants providing information about other services for which they may be eligible, including vocational rehabilitation and employment support through American Job Centers. The pilot will measure how providing information within 30 days of the initial denial notice affects short-term outcomes, such as appeal rates and timing, as well as longer-term outcomes, such as earnings, secondary appeals, and participation in vocational rehabilitation programs. The letters were mailed in March 2015. Final results including estimates of impacts on earnings are expected in February 2018.

Job Training

The Federal Government offers a number of job-training programs to help a diverse population of individuals, including military families, develop the skills they need to get on a better career path or to accelerate progress on their existing path.[94] Compared with their civilian counterparts, military spouses are significantly more likely to be unemployed or underemployed and to make less income.[95] To help close this gap, the Office of the Deputy Assistant Secretary of Defense for Military Community and Family Policy (MC&FP) established the My Career Advancement Account (MyCAA), a workforce-development program that provides up to $4,000 in tuition assistance to eligible military spouses for the pursuit of a license, credential, or

Associate Degree. MC&FP and SBST collaborated on a project to promote access to MyCAA for over 205,000 military spouses. In July 2016, MC&FP sent postcards to military spouses highlighting promising jobs and informing recipients of the large number of spouses who have already used MyCAA to kick-start a career.[96] Full results of this project are expected in late 2016.

Labor Market Information

Another way that Federal and state agencies support job seekers, businesses, and educational institutions is by providing detailed, up-to-date information about jobs, skills, and the changing nature of work. To create an easy access point for data on jobs, skills, training, and wages, DOL has partnered with the University of Chicago on the *DataAtWork* project. *DataAtWork* pools data from partner employers and other sources, employs advanced analytical techniques to generate a granular and current understanding of what kinds of skills are being supplied and demanded, and makes the results available as an open resource. SBST has teamed up with *DataAtWork* to conduct research to help ensure that this information is presented in a way that is meaningful to potential users, including workers and job seekers. SBST is interviewing leading employers, private-sector partners, state governments, and community actors who are devoted to educating and helping disadvantaged populations. This research will also facilitate the development of tools that can better match people to training opportunities and job openings that fit their unique needs and skills.

---

94 See: for example: www.whitehouse.gov/ready-to-work.

95 Rosalinda Maury and Brice Stone, "Military Spouse Employment Report," (Syracuse, N.Y.: Institute for Veterans and Military Families, February 2014).

96 John B. F. De Wit, Enny Das, and Raymond Vet, "What Works Best: Objective Statistics or a Personal Testimonial? An Assessment of the Persuasive Effects of Different Types of Message Evidence on Risk Perception," *Health Psychology* 27 (2008): 110–115; Hunt Allcott, "Social Norms and Energy Conservation," *Journal of Public Economics* 95 (2011): 1082–1095; Michael Hallsworth, John A. List, Robert D. Metcalfe, and Ivo Vlaev, "The Behavioralist as Tax Collector: Using Natural Field Experiments to Enhance Tax Compliance," (NBER Working Paper No. 20007, 2014).

Helping Families Get Health Coverage and Stay Healthy

Physical and mental health is a central element of well-being and carries significant social and economic implications for American society. A variety of Federal Government programs exist to advance the health of the Nation, including those that prevent disease, ensure food safety, offer health care to military service members and veterans, and make health insurance affordable.

Behavioral science insights have implications for health insurance programs, public health outcomes, and system and provider reforms. For example, behavioral science research informs our understanding of the underlying factors that contribute to the functioning and efficiency of health insurance markets—for example, how and why people choose one plan over others and how those choices in the aggregate may influence plan prices and availability.[97] With respect to health outcomes, research shows, for example, that simply asking people to make a specific plan to get their flu shots significantly increases vaccination rates.[98] Other research demonstrates how behavioral insights can help medical providers reduce inappropriate antibiotic prescribing.[99]

Over the past year, SBST has worked across the Federal Government to help individuals obtain and choose health insurance plans, to help keep families safe from health risks such as lead in water and food-borne illness, to increase the efficiency and operational effectiveness of health systems, and to improve child- and maternal-health outcomes worldwide.

Health Insurance Take-Up and Choice

Tens of millions of Americans now enroll in and choose health insurance coverage through Federal programs that offer a selection of private plans. In a 2015 pilot, SBST and the Center for Medicare & Medicaid Services (CMS) applied behavioral insights to increase applications for health insurance under the Affordable Care Act (ACA).[100] In the past year, SBST has been developing strategies to improve participation and support consumer choice in the Health Insurance Marketplace created by ACA, the Medicare Part D prescription drug benefit (Part D), and the Federal Employees Health Benefits (FEHB) program.

Health Insurance Take-Up

Health insurance programs that require individuals to enroll voluntarily, such as the ACA and Part D, can face take-up challenges. The Department of Health and Human Services (HHS) and SBST have led a series of efforts to increase access to ACA plans. One project focused on helping people follow through on signing up through the Federal Health Insurance Marketplace for coverage near the close of the 2015 enrollment period. With roughly two weeks remaining before the close of the open enrollment period, millions of people had visited HealthCare.gov and started an online account, but had not yet submitted an application or selected a plan. HHS, in collaboration with SBST, developed, sent, and tested variations of emails to assist these individuals with enrolling in health care coverage.

One pilot test, for example, was conducted 3 days before the open enrollment deadline. Randomly assigned individuals who had registered for a Health-Care.gov user account, but not yet enrolled in an insurance plan, were sent one of two email variants encouraging them to enroll. The email variants framed the time left until the deadline either as "3 days" (emphasizing the small number of days remaining) or "72 hours" (emphasizing urgency by using hours as the unit of time) in the email subject and body. Slightly more individuals who received the email framed as 72 hours opened the email—8.0 compared with 7.7 percent for the email framed as

97 Benjamin R. Handel, "Adverse Selection and Inertia in Health Insurance Markets: When Nudging Hurts." *American Economic Review* 103 (2013): 2643–2682.

98 Katherine L. Milkman, John Beshears, James J. Choi, David Laibson, and Brigitte C. Madrian, "Using Implementation Intentions Prompts to Enhance Influenza Vaccination Rates," *Proceedings of the National Academy of Sciences*, 108 (2011):10415–10420.

99 Daniella Meeker, Jeffrey A. Linder, Craig R. Fox, Mark W. Friedberg, Stephen D. Persell, Noah J. Goldstein, Tara K. Knight, Joel W. Hay, and Jason N. Doctor, "Effect of Behavioral Interventions on Inappropriate Antibiotic Prescribing among Primary Care Practices: A Randomized Clinical Trial," JAMA 315 (2016): 562–570.

100 Social and Behavioral Sciences Team, *Annual Report*, (2015), 38.

3 days—though there were no statistically significant differences in enrollment rates.

In an ongoing effort, HHS and SBST are focused on ensuring that individuals who failed to enroll in health care coverage in past years are aware of their options in future years. The ACA requires each individual to have a minimum level of health coverage, to qualify for an exemption, or to pay a penalty when filing taxes. About 8 million families paid an average penalty of $210 for lack of coverage in 2014, the first year the provision was implemented.[101] During the open-enrollment period for 2017 coverage, HHS will provide individuals who paid a penalty in the previous year with information about coverage options and details on how to apply. SBST is contributing to the design of these messages and a pilot test of their relative effectiveness. The pilot will examine, for example, whether emphasizing the magnitude of the penalty or the impending deadline for signing up leads to different responses among recipients.[102]

Finally, the Social Security Administration (SSA) and SBST are working to increase take-up of the Low-Income Subsidy (LIS), a premium subsidy under Part D that is worth an average of $4,000 per year for qualifying individuals.[103] Many LIS recipients are automatically enrolled in the benefit, by virtue of qualifying for Medicaid or other means-tested programs. Other qualifying individuals, however, must apply to receive the benefit, and take-up rates among this group are low: A 2010 report estimated that as many as 2.3 million Medicare beneficiaries who may be eligible for LIS are not receiving the benefit.[104] SBST and SSA are identifying opportunities to increase LIS take-up within this population.

Health Insurance Plan Choice

Health insurance is a complex product, and plans differ along multiple and sometimes hard-to-understand dimensions such as premiums, copays, and provider networks. Behavioral science underscores the challenge of presenting and structuring health insurance choices in ways that help individuals and families identify the plan that best satisfies their needs, while preserving the efficiency of these markets.[105]

Under the ACA, individuals can select insurance coverage offered by private insurers through marketplaces run by the Federal and state governments. Last year, 12.7 million individuals and families selected a health insurance plan through a marketplace.[106] While plans are grouped into metallic tiers (bronze, silver, gold, and platinum) corresponding to their level of coverage, evidence suggests that consumers may still face difficulties with plan choice.[107] To help address this issue, HHS and SBST are working to streamline plan presentation and facilitate choices within the Federal Health Insurance Marketplace.

The Medicare Part D prescription drug benefit also offers individuals the chance to select from among multiple plans. Over 41 million Medicare beneficiaries were enrolled in Part D plans in 2015.[108] Many of these

---

101 Ithai Lurie and Janet McCubbin, "What Can Tax Data Tell Us About the Uninsured? Evidence from 2014," (Working Paper, 2016).

102 Daniel Kahneman and Amos Tversky, "Prospect Theory: An Analysis of Decision Under Risk," *Econometrica* 47 (1979): 263–291; Dan Ariely and Klaus Wertenbroch, "Procrastination, Deadlines, and Performance: Self-Control by Precommitment," Psychological Science 13 (2002): 219–224.

103 Social Security Administration, *Understanding the Extra Help with your Medicare Prescription Drug Plan* (2016), https://www.ssa.gov/pubs/EN-05-10508.pdf.

104 Laura Summer, Jack Hoadley, and Elizabeth Hargrave, "The Medicare Part D Low-Income Subsidy Program: Experience to Date and Policy Issues for Consideration," (Kaiser Family Foundation, 2010).

105 Benjamin R. Handel and Jonathan T. Kolstad, "Health Insurance for 'Humans': Information Frictions, Plan Choice, and Consumer Welfare," *American Economic Review* 105 (2015): 2449–2500; Saurabh Bhargava, George Loewenstein, Justin Sydnor, "Do Individuals Make Sensible Health Insurance Decisions? Evidence from a Menu with Dominated Options," (NBER Working Paper No. 21160, 2015); Eric J. Johnson, Ran Hassin, Tom Baker, Allison T. Bajger, and Galen Treuer, "Can Consumers Make Affordable Care Affordable? The Value of Choice Architecture," *PLoS ONE* 8 (2013): e81521.

106 See: https://www.cms.gov/Newsroom/MediaReleaseDatabase/Fact-sheets/2016-Fact-sheets-items/2016-02-04.html.

107 See: https://www.healthcare.gov/choose-a-plan/plans-categories/; Peter A. Ubel, David A. Comerford, and Eric Johnson, "Healthcare.gov 3.0 — Behavioral Economics and Insurance Exchanges," *New England Journal of Medicine* 372 (2015): 695–698.

108 The Boards of Trustees of the Federal Hospital Insurance and Federal Supplementary Medical Insurance Trust Funds, *2016 Annual Report of the Boards of Trustees of the Federal Hospital Insurance and Federal Supplementary Medical Insurance Trust Funds*, (June 22, 2016).

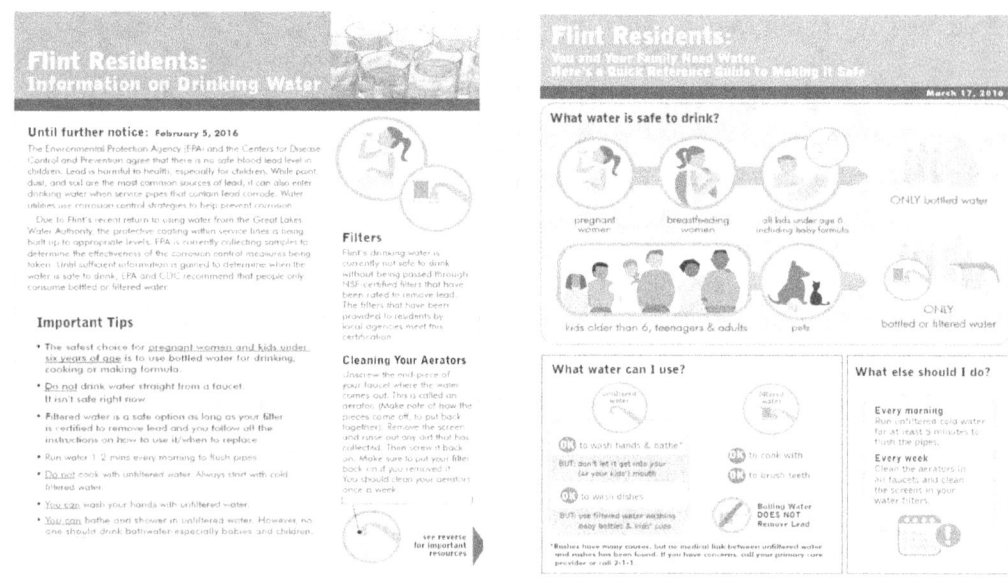

Figure 14: Informational Flyers Distributed in Flint, Michigan

Notes: An example of a modified flyer for Flint families. The original version of the flyer is on the left, and the modified flyer increasing the use of action language and visual aids is on the right.

individuals could potentially reduce their plan costs or improve their plan quality by choosing a different plan, but many do not switch: on average only 13 percent switched plans each year between 2006 and 2010.[109] Research indicates that improved decision-support for these beneficiaries could help them save about $100 per year, and better initial assignment to plans among low-income beneficiaries could potentially save the Federal Government up to $5 billion per year.[110] CMS and SBST are developing strategies to make the option

of switching plans and the benefits of doing so more salient for beneficiaries.

Finally, SBST is working with the Office of Personnel Management to update the tools available to Federal employees when they select health insurance plans in the FEHB program. The tools could allow for customized comparisons and sorting to help beneficiaries select the plans that best meet their individual needs.

Public Health

Behavioral insights can also be applied within programs that address public health issues directly. Over the past year, SBST has worked with agencies to help minimize exposure when lead is found in drinking water, develop information to reduce the risk of food-borne illness, curb inappropriate prescribing by physicians, and support the health of ill and wounded service members and their caregivers.

109 Jason Abaluck and Jonathan Gruber, "Choice Inconsistencies among the Elderly: Evidence from Plan Choice in the Medicare Part D Program," *American Economic Review*, 101 (2011): 1180–1210; Jack Hoadley, Elizabeth Hargrave, Laura Summer, Juliette Cubanski, and Tricia Neuman, "To Switch or Not to Switch: Are Medicare Beneficiaries Switching Drug Plans to Save Money?," (Kaiser Family Foundation, 2013).

110 Jeffrey R. Kling, Sendhil Mullainathan, Eldar Shafir, Lee Vermeulen, and Marian Wrobel, "Comparison Friction: Experimental Evidence from Medicare Drug Plans," *Quarterly Journal of Economics* 127 (2012): 199–235; Yuting Zhang, Chao Zhou, and Seo Hyon Baik, "A Simple Change to Medicare Part D's Low-Income Subsidy Program Could Save $5 Billion." *Health Affairs* 33 (2014): 940–945.

Lead exposure can result in severe health consequences, especially for children.[111] Since early 2016, the Federal Government has been responding to the risks posed by elevated lead levels in the water in Flint, Michigan.[112] A central component of this effort has been to get clear, actionable information on reducing lead exposure into the hands of Flint residents quickly.[113] The Environmental Protection Agency (EPA) and SBST redesigned outreach and educational materials for Flint residents, drawing on the best available evidence of how to communicate information and prompt action. As illustrated in Figure 14, SBST reduced the amount of text in the flyers, provided answers to key questions, and organized recommended actions by their frequency (daily versus weekly).[114] SBST and EPA continue to collaborate on further outreach to members of the Flint community to empower them with up-to-date information and evidence-based recommendations.

Building on this work, SBST is exploring a broader collaboration with EPA to evaluate and improve the effectiveness of information provided about lead in water nationwide.

In another public health effort, SBST is addressing the dangers posed by foodborne illness. Approximately 48 million cases of foodborne illness occur in the United States each year, resulting in roughly 128,000 hospitalizations and 3,000 deaths.[115] Providing information to consumers on safe food handling and preparation practices is one way of minimizing foodborne haz-

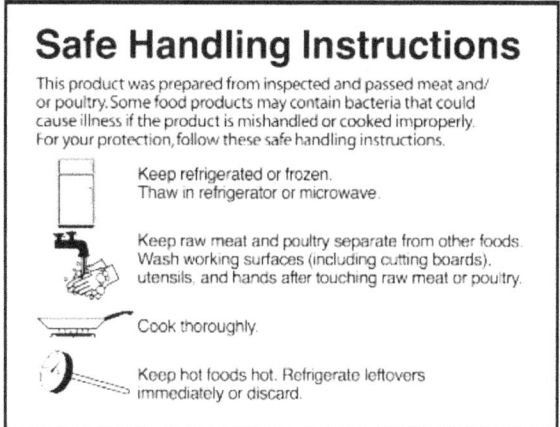

Figure 15: Safe Handling Instructions label

Notes: The current Safe Handling Instructions label.

ards. To this end, the U.S. Department of Agriculture's (USDA) Food Safety and Inspection Service (FSIS) has developed a Safe Handling Instructions (SHI) label, which is required on any raw or partially cooked and not ready-to-eat meat or poultry product (see Figure 15).[116] SBST is partnering with FSIS to redesign the SHI label using evidence from behavioral science about the most effective way to communicate risk information and motivate subsequent action.

Inappropriate prescribing of pharmaceutical drugs threatens patients' health and increases the cost of health care. Through its Center for Program Integrity (CPI), CMS uses a variety of approaches to combat overprescribing behavior, such as proactively identifying providers suspected of inappropriate activity and pursuing legal action through law enforcement channels. Using lessons learned from an ineffective letter campaign targeting opioid prescriptions in 2014, CPI, SBST, and academic researchers have redesigned the original intervention and are testing its impact on inappropriate prescriptions of a common antipsychotic. The redesign includes emphasizing the negative consequences of inappropriate prescriber behavior, sending the letters to

---

111 An NIH summary can be viewed at: http://www.niehs.nih.gov/health/materials/lead_and_your_health_508.pdf.

112 See: https://www.epa.gov/flint.

113 See: https://www.whitehouse.gov/the-press-office/2016/05/03/fact-sheet-federal-support-flint-water-crisis-response-and-recovery.

114 W. Howard Levie and Richard Lentz, "Effects of Text Illustrations: A Review of Research," *Educational Communication and Technology*, 30 (1982): 195–232; Sav Shrestha, Kelsi Lenz, Barbara Chaparro, and Justin Owens, "'F' Pattern Scanning of Text and Images in Web Pages," *Proceedings of the Human Factors and Ergonomics Society Annual Meeting*, 51 (2007): 1200–1204.

115 See: CDC statistics on foodborne illness at: https://www.cdc.gov/foodborneburden.

116 Labels: definition; required features, *Code of Federal Regulations*, title 9, part 317.2 (2011): 173–174, https://www.gpo.gov/fdsys/pkg/CFR-2011-title9-vol2/pdf/CFR-2011-title9-vol2-sec317-2.pdf.

prescribers multiple times, relying on more recent data on prescriber behavior rather than data from previous years, and accessing more accurate prescriber mailing addresses.[117] Results of this pilot are forthcoming.

Military Caregiver Forums

To support individuals caring for ill and wounded service members, the Department of Defense sponsors virtual PEER (Personalized Experiences, Education, and Resources) forums, which provide an opportunity for those caring for ill and wounded service members to meet remotely and share knowledge and resources and receive social and emotional support. DOD and SBST have collaborated to increase awareness and utilization of these forums, sending outreach emails to thousands of caregivers, and testing the relative effects of emails emphasizing the forums as a way for caregivers to either "get support" or "give support" to their peers. Preliminary results show that emails with the "get support" message had a slightly higher open rate than the "give support" message. In addition, SBST designed an interactive web-based activity to encourage individuals to engage more actively with the program.

Health Systems

Behavioral insights also hold the promise of making health systems more efficient and cost effective. For example, electronic health records (EHRs) can yield benefits for both patients and providers.[118] CMS offers incentives, provides information, and gives target usage metrics to healthcare providers to encour-age adoption of EHRs.[119] The Office of the National Coordinator for Health Information Technology (ONC) and SBST partnered with a regional health care system to increase utilization of online patient portals through revised information and clear action steps given to patients in a paper After Visit Summary.[120] This intervention was estimated to lead to a 10 percentage point increase in the likelihood of online patient portal account activation, though the estimate was imprecise by conventional standards ($p=.07$).

SBST is also collaborating with the Defense Health Agency's (DHA) Patient Centered Medical Home (PCMH) Office and the Navy Hospital (NH) Camp Lejeune Family Medicine Clinic to promote secure messaging through online health portals between providers and patients using personal appeals, staff assistance in registration, and follow-up reminders. The project launched in July of 2016, and results will be used to inform guidance for all U.S. Military medical treatment facilities nationwide.

Global Health

The United States Agency for International Development (USAID) has strong precedents for applying evidence-based behavioral interventions to improve programs, save lives, and scale what is most effective. For example, USAID/Mozambique and partners scaled up the successful SMS Saúde study, which found that urban HIV patients who had just started treatment and received a SMS reminder to take their medicine and attend doctor's appointments were significantly more likely to stay on the treatment and live longer. [121]

117 Lucio Castro and Carlos Scartascini, "Tax Compliance and Enforcement in the Pampas," (Inter-American Development Bank Working Paper No. IDB-WP-472, 2013); Gerlinde Fellner, Rupert Sausgruber, and Christian Traxler, "Testing Enforcement Strategies in the Field: Threat, Moral Appeal, and Social Information," *Journal of the European Economic Association* 11 (2013): 634–660.

118 Congressional Budget Office, *Evidence on the Costs and Benefits of Health Information Technology*, (2008); Beverly Bell and Kelly Thornton, "From Promise to Reality: Achieving the Value of an EHR: Realizing the Benefits of an EHR Requires Specific Steps to Establish Goals, Involve Physicians and Other Key Stakeholders, Improve Processes, and Manage Organizational Change," *Healthcare Financial Management* 65 (2011): 51–57.

119 See: https://www.healthit.gov/providers-professionals/meaningful-use-definition-objectives.

120 John Beshears, James J. Choi, David Laibson, and Brigitte C. Madrian, "Simplification and Saving," *Journal of Economic Behavior & Organization* 95 (2013): 130–145.

121 Dvora Joseph Davey, Nhavoto, José António; Augusto, Orvalho; Ponce, Walter; Traca, Dalia; Nguimfack, Alexandre; De Sousa, Cesar Palha, "SMSaude: Evaluating Mobile Phone Text Reminders to Improve Retention in HIV Care for Patients on Antiretroviral Therapy in Mozambique," Journal of Acquired Immune Deficiency Syndromes (forthcoming, 2016).

Since 2014, USAID and SBST have been collaborating on a series of pilots around the globe with a focus on child and maternal health. These include launching and evaluating Mozambique's first mobile-based vaccination platform that allows officials to keep track of vaccine supply and remind caregivers who have missed appointments to attend upcoming ones, and improving sanitation in India by providing additional cleaning solutions and incentivizing individuals through a lottery prize to use community toilets.

In 2016, selected USAID Missions and partners were invited to join SBST Fellows and world-class academic experts for the first ever USAID International Behavioral Design Workshop. Projects emerging from this workshop include: increasing the number of pregnant women who receive intermittent preventive treatment to reduce malaria risk by redesigning referral forms with USAID/Nigeria; increasing HIV medication adherence among high-risk populations using text message notices and transportation subsidies with USAID/Ethiopia; and offering personalized and simplified counseling on healthy pregnancies with USAID/Nigeria and their partners. Results from these studies are forthcoming.

Improving Government Effectiveness and Efficiency

Finally, SBST worked with Federal agencies over the past year to improve the effectiveness and efficiency of Government operations and program management. SBST worked to streamline tax administration, improve the efficiency of Government auctions, and strengthen Federal workforce productivity.

Tax Administration

Together with the Department of the Treasury's (Treasury) Office of Tax Policy, tax-software developers, and academic researchers, the Internal Revenue Service (IRS) is using data-driven methods to guide its administration of refundable credits. The goal of this effort is to promote compliant participation and deter systemic non-compliance. The IRS is utilizing three channels to communicate context-specific information about tax-return preparation: through tax-software developers, through tax software, and directly to the taxpayer. The IRS is also using rigorous evaluations, such as randomized control trials, to identify what information to provide to whom and at what point in the refundable claims process. For example, the IRS and Treasury collaborated with tax-software developers to test the impact of embedding multiple messages into tax-preparation software on rates of tax filing and credit claiming.

The Earned Income Tax Credit (EITC) is one of the largest refundable credits, sending over $66 billion in income assistance to more than 27 million working families in 2015, while encouraging additional workforce participation.[122] While EITC participation rates among eligible households are relatively high, at 75 percent, millions of individuals—many of whom do not have children—who may be eligible do not claim the credit each year, either because

they file their returns but do not claim the credit, or because they do not file at all.[123] The IRS, academic researchers, and General Services Administration (GSA) members of SBST tested the impact of mailing notices about tax filing and EITC participation to potentially eligible individuals who did not file a tax return in recent years.[124] Six variants of postcards and brochures that highlighted the benefits of the EITC were sent to individuals.[125] The notices resulted in a modest, but statistically significant, increase in the rate of tax filing (37.8 compared to 36.8 percent), which in turn increased EITC filing rates. Conditional on filing, there were no significant differences in the fraction of individuals claiming the EITC, suggesting that the primary barrier to increasing EITC claims for this population is getting individuals to file a return.

A related project focused on increasing take-up of tax benefits that support higher education, such as the American Opportunity Tax Credit (AOTC).[126] While these tax benefits are available to college students to offset the costs of post-secondary education, students may fail to realize their eligibility or take the necessary actions to claim the credit.[127] To address this issue, researchers at the IRS, Treasury, and GSA members of SBST sent informational notices during the 2015 tax filing season to quali-

122 See: https://www.eitc.irs.gov/EITC-Central/eitcstats. For a recent review and discussion of the labor supply effects of the EITC, see: Bruce Meyer, "The Effects of the Earned Income Tax Credit and Recent Reforms," in Jeffrey R. Brown, ed., *Tax Policy and the Economy* (NBER, 2010).

123 Dean Plueger, "Earned Income Tax Credit Participation Rate for Tax Year 2005," (IRS Working Paper, 2009).

124 For a full report on this project, see: John Guyton, Dayanand S. Manoli, Brenda Schafer, and Michael Sebastiani, "Reminders & Recidivism: Evidence from Tax Filing & EITC Participation among Low-Income Nonfilers," (NBER Working Paper No. 21904, 2016).

125 Saurabh Bhargava and Dayanand S. Manoli, "Psychological Frictions and the Incomplete Take-Up of Social Benefits: Evidence from an IRS Field Experiment," *American Economic Review* 105 (2015); Dayanand S. Manoli and Nicholas Turner, "Nudges and Learning: Evidence from Informational Interventions for Low-Income Taxpayers," (NBER Working Paper No. 20718, 2014).

126 For additional information on tax benefits for education, see: https://www.irs.gov/pub/irs-pdf/p970.pdf.

127 U.S. Government Accountability Office, *Higher Education: Improved Tax Information Could Help Families Pay for College*, GAO-12-560 (Washington, DC, 2012); George B. Bulman and Caroline M. Hoxby, "The Returns to the Federal Tax Credits for Higher Education," *Tax Policy and the Economy* 29 (2015): 13–88.

fying families who appeared eligible for the credit based on tuition (1098-T) and wage (W-2) information.[128] The impact of the notices on AOTC take-up and college attendance will be reported in forthcoming results.

Operational Efficiency

GSA sells Government agency surplus items, such as technology equipment and vehicles, to the public through an online auction site.[129] While many items for sale receive sufficient attention and bidding to ensure competitive prices, many other items do not, leading to auctions that close after little (or no) bidding activity. Underpriced and unsold golds can result in significant foregone revenue for the Government.

GSA and SBST developed a simple algorithm to identify auctions that were at risk of closing without receiving any bids. The algorithm also identified bidders who had bid on similar items in the recent past and might be interested in these items. Emails about the relevant items were sent to identified bidders and contained a picture of the item, its current price, a clickable link to view and bid on the item, and a note indicating the short timeframe remaining before the auction would close. During the period of September 2015 to March 2016, bidders who were sent emails submitted a total of 68

bids on items that were otherwise unlikely to receive any bids. More detailed results of this project are forthcoming.

Federal Workforce Productivity

Improving managerial performance and engagement is a priority across Government. To improve managerial performance and associated workplace performance outcomes, the Performance Improvement Council (PIC) and SBST developed and evaluated a new professional-development tool for Federal managers. The tool consists of an eight-module course to help managers develop eight specific traits that research finds are present in successful managers.[130] This training was delivered to a subset of managers at the Department of Labor and the Department of Energy in 2016. As a supplement to the program, SBST also designed a "growth mindset" intervention, which emphasized that managerial abilities are not fixed, but can be learned and strengthened over time.[131] Research demonstrates that promoting a growth mindset may lead managers to be more engaged with workers and support a culture that increases worker productivity.[132] This project concluded in early September 2016, and results will be made available soon.

128 John Guyton, Dayanand S. Manoli, Brenda Schafer, Michael Sebastiani, and Nicholas Turner, "Tax Knowledge and College: Do IRS Reminders Affect Tax-Based Aid Use?," (presented at the 108th National Tax Association Annual Conference on Taxation, November 21, 2015).

129 For more information on GSA auctions, see: https://gsaauctions.gov.

130 David A. Garvin, "How Google Sold Its Engineers on Management," *Harvard Business Review* (December 2013).

131 Lisa S. Blackwell, Kali H. Trzesniewski, and Carol Sorich Dweck, "Implicit Theories of Intelligence Predict Achievement across an Adolescent Transition: A Longitudinal Study and an Intervention," *Child Development* 78 (2007): 246–263.

132 Peter A. Heslin and Don VandeWalle, "Managers' Implicit Assumptions About Personnel," *Current Directions in Psychological Science* 17 (2008): 219–223.

Appendix

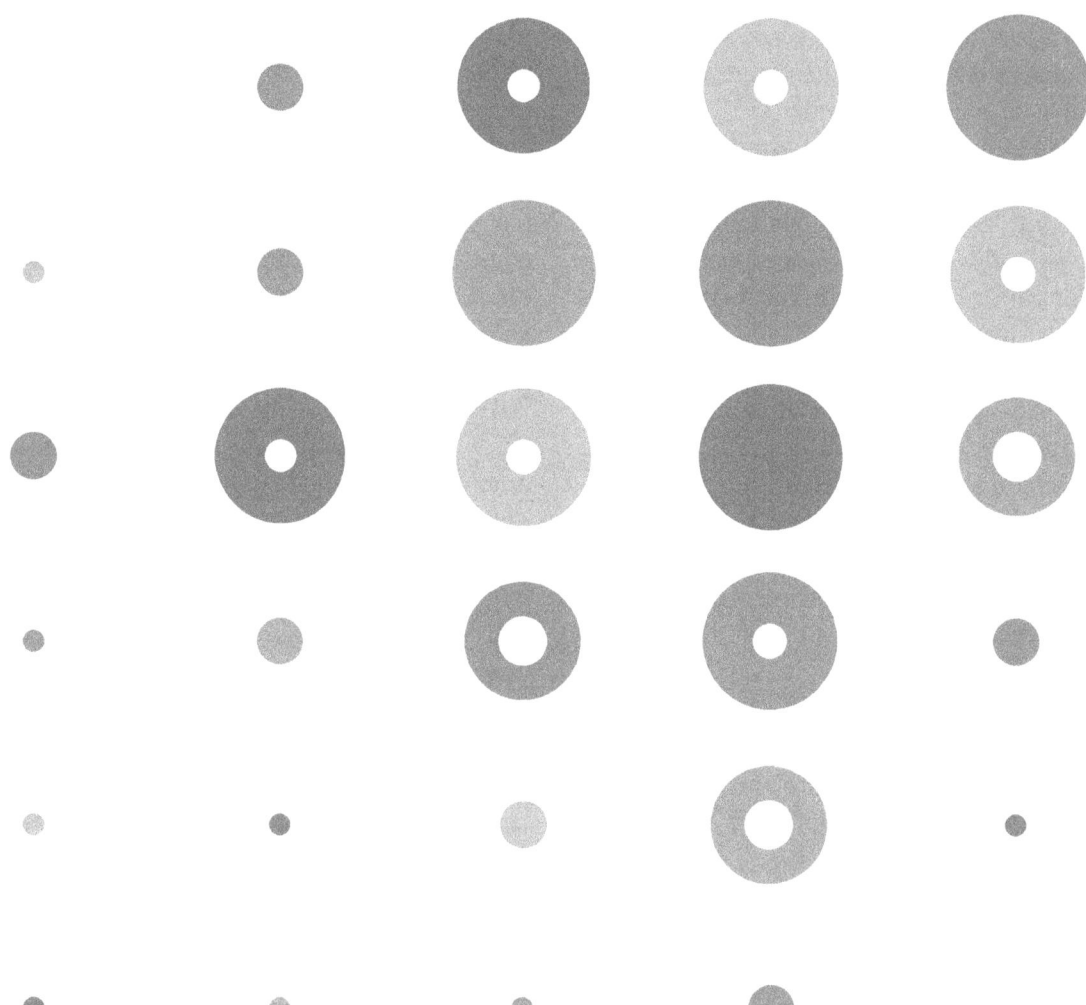

September 15, 2016

MEMORANDUM TO THE HEADS OF EXECUTIVE DEPARTMENTS AND AGENCIES

FROM: John P. Holdren
          Director

SUBJECT: Implementation Guidance for Executive Order 13707: Using Behavioral Science
          Insights to Better Serve the American People

INTRODUCTION

On September 15, 2015, President Obama issued Executive Order 13707, "Using Behavioral Science Insights to Better Serve the American People," recognizing that "behavioral science insights can support a range of national priorities, including helping workers to find better jobs; enabling Americans to lead longer, healthier lives; improving access to educational opportunities and support for success in school; and accelerating the transition to a low-carbon economy." The Executive Order calls for the Assistant to the President for Science and Technology, on behalf of the Social and Behavioral Sciences Team (SBST), to provide agencies with advice and policy guidance to help them execute the policy objectives of the Order.

This guidance document focuses on agency implementation of Section 1(a)(i) of the Order, which encourages agencies to identify promising opportunities to apply behavioral-science insights to Federal policies and programs. It is organized around four key aspects of Federal policy where research and practice show that behavioral factors play an especially strong role in program outcomes[1]: (1) determining access to programs, (2) presenting information to the public, (3) structuring choices within programs, and (4) designing incentives.

In many cases, program changes that leverage behavioral-science insights can be done under existing authorities. In cases where changes to underlying program design are required, policymakers are encouraged to consider how such changes could be accomplished while preserving overall program objectives. Agencies are encouraged to contact SBST for advice and assistance as they work in support of this directive.

DETAILED GUIDANCE

1. Access to Programs

Pursuant to section (1)(b)(i) of Executive Order 13707, agencies are encouraged to "identify opportunities to help qualifying individuals, families, communities, and businesses access public programs and benefits by, as appropriate, streamlining processes that may otherwise limit or delay participation—for example, removing administrative hurdles, shortening wait times, and simplifying forms."

---

[1] Raj Chetty, "Behavioral Economics and Public Policy: A Pragmatic Perspective," *American Economic Review* 105 (2015): 1–33; Brigitte C. Madrian, "Applying Insights from Behavioral Economics to Policy Design," *Annual Review of Economics* 6 (2014): 663–688; Eldar Shafir, ed., *The Behavioral Foundations of Public Policy*, (Princeton, 2012); William J. Congdon, Jeffrey R. Kling, and Sendhil Mullainathan, *Policy and Choice Public Finance through the Lens of Behavioral Economics*, (Brookings Institution, 2011); Richard H. Thaler and Cass R. Sunstein, *Nudge* (Yale, 2008).

The Federal Government administers a wide array of programs on behalf of the American people. Well-known examples include financial aid to assist with college attendance, social-insurance programs and tax benefits to promote retirement security, and health-insurance programs to ensure access to healthcare and financial protection for families.

Access to these programs and benefits is typically determined by defined eligibility criteria and a specified process by which individuals apply for programs, claim benefits, or maintain their participation. Behavioral-science research shows that even small barriers imposed by program rules and procedures can have outsized impacts on program access and outcomes. As such, when agencies are determining the rules and procedures that govern access to their programs, they should consider streamlining access for eligible individuals.

1.1. Central insight: Small barriers to program access can have large impacts on participation and outcomes

Behavioral-science insights suggest that imperfect take-up in Federal programs may not necessarily reflect a lack of interest in those programs among eligible individuals. Instead, low take-up may result from barriers to program access that deter eligible people from participating.[2] Potential barriers include the length and complexity of applications and forms, the length of wait times to speak or meet with program officials, travel or time costs associated with application processes, and overly burdensome verification requirements. By negatively affecting program participation, these small barriers can prevent programs from delivering their intended social or economic benefits.[3]

Note that while a standard economic analysis suggests that the costs associated with program access—whether in time, hassle, or otherwise—can lead to efficient screening (i.e., those individuals who will benefit most from a program will find the costs associated with participation most worth paying), a behavioral perspective recognizes that this may not always be the case. In fact, those individuals who would most benefit from a program may be among those most affected by small barriers and minor costs.[4] As a result, agencies should be aware that eligible non-participants are not necessarily those individuals who value the program the least.

1.2. Key Implication: Agencies should consider streamlining access to programs

1.2.1. *Consider streamlining processes for enrolling in programs, such as by simplifying forms or making use of available administrative data*

Agencies should consider opportunities to simplify the process by which eligible individuals access programs and benefits. Forms can be shortened and simplified, and technology can be used to make forms accessible through a variety of channels, such as online.[5] For example, research has shown that a lengthy Free Application for Federal Student Aid (FAFSA) not only discouraged students from applying for aid, but also led some students to delay or forgo college altogether. When researchers provided families with application assistance and helped them to fill out parts of the application using information from their tax

[2] Marianne Bertrand, Sendhil Mullainathan, and Eldar Shafir, "Behavioral Economics and Marketing in Aid of Decision Making Among the Poor," *Journal of Public Policy & Marketing* 25 (2006): 8–23.

[3] Of note: on March 30, 2016, the Office of Management and Budget (OMB) launched the Core Federal Services Council, which comprises the top 30 or so Federal programs that provide services directly to the public. The Council promotes the use of customer-centric best practices and has conducted a self-assessment identifying design as a critical discipline to improve the delivery of services. See, OMB Memo M 16-08 (Establishment of the Core Federal Services Council) at: https://www.whitehouse.gov/sites/default/files/omb/memoranda/2016/m-16-08.pdf

[4] Anuj K. Shah, Sendhil Mullainathan, and Eldar Shafir, "Some Consequences of Having Too Little," *Science*, 338 (2012): 682–685.

[5] See the joint OIRA and OSTP memorandum of September 15, 2015: "Behavioral Science Insights and Federal Forms": www.whitehouse.gov/sites/default/files/omb/inforeg/memos/2015/behavioral-science-insights-and-federal-forms.pdf as well as the OMB memorandum of August 9, 2012: "Testing and Simplifying Federal Forms": www.whitehouse.gov/sites/default/files/omb/inforeg/memos/testing-and-simplifying-federal-forms.pdf

return, it increased rates of FAFSA applications as well as college enrollment and matriculation.[6] Based in part on this research, the Department of Education (ED) has taken a series of steps to streamline the FAFSA, enabling applicants to skip questions that don't pertain to them and to automatically fill parts of the application using information from their tax return.[7]

Agencies can also use existing administrative data—such as by making eligibility determinations for one program based on data available under other programs—to streamline program access. Direct certification for low-income students into the National School Lunch Program (NSLP) based on their eligibility for the Supplemental Nutrition Assistance Program (SNAP) or Medicaid is one example.[8] Agencies can also create channels that allow individuals to draw on administrative data directly to reduce barriers to access, as in the case of financial-aid applicants populating the FAFSA with data from their income tax return.

1.2.2. *Consider automatically enrolling eligible individuals*

Where possible, agencies can use default program settings to encourage participation. Research has found, for example, that individuals are substantially more likely to participate in and save through retirement plans when they are automatically enrolled in those plans and their contribution rates escalate automatically.[9] Reflecting this research, the Pension Protection Act (PPA) of 2006 facilitates the practice of automatically enrolling workers into retirement-savings plans.[10]

1.2.3. *Consider the impact of enrollment or application periods on program participation*

For programs where access is only available at discrete points in time (e.g., health-insurance programs with annual enrollment periods, financial-aid application timelines that reflect school calendars, or benefits that are claimed as part of tax filing), agencies can help ensure that application windows and deadlines are set up to promote access. When individuals' financial resources and available time are not well-aligned with enrollment timelines, it may be more difficult for individuals to complete the administrative processes required to establish or maintain participation in a program.[11] For example, forthcoming changes by ED will allow students to apply for financial aid earlier in the school year. This change will allow students to use expected levels of financial support to inform their decisions about whether and where to apply to college, which may in turn support college access.[12]

1.2.4. *Consider revisiting program-eligibility criteria in cases where the benefits to targeting efficiency may be outweighed by the costs to program access and outcomes*

While program application requirements, such as questions on a form, might represent a barrier to access, they typically serve the function of collecting necessary information to determine benefit eligibility. The marginal benefit of such questions (i.e., improving targeting efficiency) should be weighed against the marginal cost (i.e., deterring access). A key implication from behavioral science is that failing to take

---

[6] Eric P. Bettinger, Bridget Terry Long, Philip Oreopoulos, and Lisa Sanbonmatsu, "The Role of Application Assistance and Information in College Decisions: Results from the H&R Block Fafsa Experiment," *Quarterly Journal of Economics* 127 (2012): 1205–1242.

[7] U.S. Department of Education, "Fiscal Year 2017 Budget: Summary and Background Information," (2016), p. 46.

[8] Direct certification refers to the ability of states and local education authorities to certify children as eligible for the NSLP without the need for an application by using information that those authorities have, such as whether or not a household receives Supplemental Nutrition Assistance Program benefits. For more information on direct certification in NSLP, see: "Direct Certification in the National School Lunch Program: State Implementation Progress, School Year 2012–2013," U.S. Department of Agriculture (2013), p. 2.

[9] Brigitte C. Madrian and Dennis F. Shea, "The Power of Suggestion: Inertia in 401(k) Participation and Savings Behavior," *Quarterly Journal of Economics* 116 (2001): 1149–1187; Richard H. Thaler and Shlomo Benartzi, "Save More Tomorrow™: Using Behavioral Economics to Increase Employee Saving," *Journal of Political Economy* 112 (2004): S164–S187.

[10] Pension Protection Act of 2006, Public Law 109-280, U.S. Statutes at Large 120 (2006): 780–1172.

[11] Katherine Swartz and John A. Graves, "Shifting The Open Enrollment Period For ACA Marketplaces Could Increase Enrollment And Improve Plan Choices," *Health Affairs*, June 25, 2014.

[12] See a description of this change the FAFSA application timeline at: https://studentaid.ed.gov/sa/about/announcements/fafsa-changes

these costs into account can lead to eligibility criteria that are more burdensome than necessary.[13] For example, in the case of financial aid, the costs of having a complex application include deterring or delaying some students from attending college. Agencies and policymakers should consider whether underlying eligibility rules are optimal. Consider again the example of the FAFSA: research suggests that even a substantial reduction in the amount of information required of applicants would have relatively small impacts on the ability of the program to efficiently target aid to those most in need.[14]

Note, too, that small differences in eligibility criteria across programs can prevent agencies from using administrative data to cross-enroll individuals into other programs without requiring a duplicative collection of information.[15] Where possible, agencies should align eligibility criteria or adopt standard definitions of key fields, such as income or family size, across programs that are meant to serve similar or overlapping populations.

Finally, while important for program integrity, frequent or burdensome recertification requirements may impede eligible individuals' continued participation in programs. Agencies can utilize similar tools for reducing these barriers as they might for initial program applications. For example, agencies can draw on administrative data sources, simplify processes, or consider the timing of recertification periods by aligning them with those of other programs.

2. <u>Information provision</u>

Section (1)(b)(ii) of Executive Order 13707 encourages agencies to "improve how information is presented to consumers, borrowers, program beneficiaries, and other individuals, whether as directly conveyed by the agency, or in setting standards for the presentation of information, by considering how the content, format, timing, and medium by which information is conveyed affects comprehension and action by individuals, as appropriate."

Agencies issue informational products to the public directly, provide data and statistics through websites and other formats, and enforce labeling and disclosure standards that apply to businesses. Examples include the nutrition facts label found on packaged foods, the mortgage disclosures presented to borrowers at settlement, the Energy Star label on consumer appliances, and the College Scorecard.[16] Well-presented information makes it easier for consumers to satisfy their preferences and make informed choices, in addition to supporting the efficient functioning of markets.

As such, it is important that agencies consider not just the accuracy and completeness of the information they provide to the public, but also how individuals are likely to understand and respond to that information.

2.1. Central insight: How individuals understand and respond to information depends on its presentation

Behavioral science research demonstrates that how people understand and act on information depends not only on the quality and completeness of that information, but also on the manner in which it is presented. The complexity of information, the units and scale with which numerical information is presented,

---

[13] Henrik Jacobsen Kleven and Wojciech Kopczuk, "Transfer Program Complexity and the Take-Up of Social Benefits," *American Economic Journal Economic Policy* 3 (2011): 54–90.

[14] Susan M. Dynarski and Judith E. Scott-Clayton, "College Grants on a Postcard: A Proposal for Simple and Predictable Federal Student Aid," Hamilton Project Discussion Paper 2007-01 (Brookings, 2007); Kim S. Rueben, Sarah Gault, Sandy Baum, "Simplifying Federal Student Aid: How Do the Plans Stack Up?," (Urban Institute, November 2015).

[15] Stan Dorn, "Integrating Health and Human Services Programs and Reaching Eligible Individuals under the Affordable Care Act: Final Report," Report Prepared for the Department of Health and Human Services, (Urban Institute, February 2015).

[16] The College Scorecard can be viewed at: https://collegescorecard.ed.gov/

whether information is framed as a loss or gain, how probabilities are communicated, and other elements of the presentation all strongly contribute to how individuals interpret and respond to information.[17]

2.2. Key implication: Agencies should present information in a manner that is meaningful to the intended audience and that effectively promotes the intended use of that information

2.2.1. *Consider the salience of the information provided*

The salience of information—how readily it commands attention—can affect how individuals interpret and act on the content. Simplified notices that make program benefits salient have helped qualifying individuals claim the Earned Income Tax Credit.[18] Agencies should also consider the location and timing of where and when information will be encountered by decision-makers, in relation to the location and timing of the decision or action that information is intended to inform. For example, information intended to help consumers make purchasing decisions may be more effective when it is presented at the time of purchase, as with nutrition labeling.[19] Finally, agencies should consider the overall amount, density, and mix of information being presented, along with its format, specificity, and content.

2.2.2. *Consider the framing of the information provided*

Agencies are encouraged to consider how alternative ways of presenting the same information can affect how individuals understand and act on it. When presenting numerical or probabilistic information, for example, research shows that two mathematically equivalent expressions can lead to different levels of understanding and different actions. In one study, the presentation of automotive fuel efficiency in gallons per mile, rather than miles per gallon, led individuals to form more accurate judgments about the relative benefits of alternative automotive purchases.[20] Based in part on this research, the sticker required by the Environmental Protection Agency to display fuel efficiency on new cars, which traditionally described fuel efficiency in terms of miles per gallon, now also presents the same information in gallons per mile.[21]

Where information is provided to foster comparisons, agencies should carefully consider the use of units, scales, and reference points. For example, presenting interest rates as an annual percentage rate rather than a biweekly fee has been shown to decrease the use of high-cost payday loans.[22] Agencies can also use personalized information and illustrative examples to more effectively communicate information. For example, the Card Accountability Responsibility and Disclosure Act requires that credit card statements indicate the interest savings from paying off full balances in 36 months rather than simply making the minimum required payment.[23]

3. Choices within programs

Section (1)(b)(iii) of Executive Order 13707 encourages agencies to "identify programs that offer choices and carefully consider how the presentation and structure of those choices, including the order, number,

---

[17] Daniel Kahneman and Amos Tversky, "Prospect Theory: An Analysis of Decision under Risk," *Econometrica* 47 (1979): 263–291; Marianne Bertrand, Dean Karlan, Sendhil Mullainathan, Eldar Shafir, and Jonathan Zinman, "What's Advertising Content Worth? Evidence from a Consumer Credit Marketing Field Experiment," *Quarterly Journal of Economics* 125 (2010): 263–305.

[18] Saurabh Bhargava and Dayanand Manoli, "Psychological Frictions and the Incomplete Take-Up of Social Benefits: Evidence from an IRS Field Experiment," *American Economic Review* 105 (2015): 3489–3529; Dayanand S. Manoli and Nicholas Turner, "Nudges and Learning: Evidence from Informational Interventions for Low-Income Taxpayers," (NBER Working Paper No. 20718, November 2014).

[19] Jessica Wisdom, Julie S Downs, and George Loewenstein, "Promoting Healthy Choices: Information versus Convenience," *American Economic Journal Applied Economics* 2 (2010): 164–178.

[20] Richard P Larrick and Jack B. Soll, "The MPG Illusion," *Science* 320 (2008): 1593–1594.

[21] Cass R. Sunstein, *Simpler The Future of Government*, (New York: Simon & Schuster, 2013).

[22] Marianne Bertrand and Adair Morse, "Information Disclosure, Cognitive Biases, and Payday Borrowing," *The Journal of Finance* 66 (2011): 1865–1893.

[23] Sumit Agarwal, Souphala Chomsisengphet, Neale Mahoney, and Johannes Stroebel, "Regulating Consumer Financial Products: Evidence from Credit Cards," *Quarterly Journal of Economics* 130 (2015): 111–164.

and arrangement of options, can most effectively promote public welfare, as appropriate, giving particular consideration to the selection and setting of default options."

Many Federal policies and programs offer individuals choices. Sometimes these are choices from an explicit menu of options—for example, health-insurance plans offered by private insurers, or student-loan repayment plans. In other instances, choices are implicit in the design of the program—for example, in the retirement portion of Social Security where eligible individuals may elect to claim benefits across a range of ages.

When agencies offer choices within programs, they should consider ways to simplify the presentation and structure of different options and to assist individuals with making decisions.

3.1. Central insight: Complex or difficult choices in programs can lead individuals to choose inconsistently

Behavioral-science evidence shows that how people choose among options within a program can be sensitive to even minor features of the context in which a decision is made; that is, people are materially influenced by factors such as the complexity of the choice or the number of available options.[24] Research demonstrates that individuals can have difficulty choosing, and choosing consistently, when choices involve numerous alternatives, vary along multiple or complex dimensions, involve assessments of probability or risk, or have a substantial time dimension (i.e., choices made now that have consequences long into the future).

Importantly, the structure of program alternatives has consequences not just for the welfare of the individuals facing the choice, but also for market outcomes more broadly. For example, in Federal health-insurance programs where individual buyers select plans offered by private insurers, the efficiency of the overall marketplace depends, in part, on individual choices (to which insurers will dynamically respond). Similarly, patterns of choice can also limit the efficacy of the marketplace. For example, health insurance markets can suffer from what is known as adverse selection—individuals in relatively poor health choose more generous coverage, but their greater expected health-care expenditures can negatively affect plan pricing and availability. That said, behavioral factors, such as individuals' tendencies to stick with plan choices over time, regardless of their health status, may mediate such effects.[25]

3.2. Key implication: Agencies should improve how choices are offered in programs

3.2.1. *Where complex choices are presented in programs, consider efforts to assist individuals with making those choices*

Behavioral insights suggest that how individuals choose among Federal program options can be sensitive to how those options are presented to individuals. Research shows that people's choices in a particular context may not always reflect individual preferences, but instead reflect their difficulty choosing the option that best fits their needs. Simplifying the presentation of choices or assisting individuals with making choices might benefit individuals and support program objectives.

Agencies can assist individuals with making choices by better communicating and presenting information about options and consequences. For example, it has been shown that individuals are more likely to

---

[24] Eric J. Johnson, Suzanne B. Shu, Benedict G. C. Dellaert, Craig Fox, Daniel G. Goldstein, Gerald Häubl, Richard P. Larrick, et al., "Beyond Nudges: Tools of a Choice Architecture," *Marketing Letters* 23 (2012): 487–504.
[25] Benjamin R. Handel, "Adverse Selection and Inertia in Health Insurance Markets: When Nudging Hurts," *American Economic Review* 103 (2013): 2643–2682.

choose the first item from a list or the first option they consider.[26] Therefore, agencies should consider carefully the order in which options are presented on forms, on websites, or in other materials.

To facilitate easier choices, options can be grouped into meaningful categories as seen in the metallic tiers used to organize plans in the Health Insurance Marketplace (bronze, silver, gold, and platinum), which correspond to their generosity of coverage.[27] Personalizing information can also help support individual choices. For example, in one study, offering beneficiaries personalized information about costs among Medicare Part D prescription drug plans led recipients to choose lower-cost plans.[28]

Agencies should also consider developing or promoting the use of decision-support tools, sometimes known as choice engines, to help individuals make decisions when program choices are complex.[29] These could include adaptive tools that help individuals to narrow, sort, or personalize options based on their circumstances or preferences. For example, the Medicare Plan Finder allows beneficiaries to project their costs under multiple Medicare Part D prescription drug plan options based on information they enter regarding their geographic location and the prescription drugs they are currently taking. Decision tools can also leverage existing program administrative data to provide more personalized, automated recommendations to individuals. Finally, agencies can support the creation of such tools not only by building them directly, but by encouraging private-sector innovation. Disclosing information in machine readable formats can enable use of third-party tools or choice engines developed by the private sector.[30]

3.2.2. *Review opportunities to use default settings or require active choices to assist individuals*

Agencies should review how default choices are set within programs. Behavioral science suggests that individuals tend to stick with default settings, as demonstrated by their effectiveness in retirement savings plans.[31] Importantly, setting defaults can reduce choice complexity without reducing the total number of options available to individuals, thereby assisting individuals and advancing program goals.

In some circumstances, no single default setting is appropriate or suitable for every individual covered by a program. In such cases, defaults can sometimes be personalized to individual circumstances and characteristics.[32] For example, in health-insurance programs, individuals can be presented with defaults tailored to their personal or family circumstances based on program data or data they have entered.[33] Default settings can also have dynamic features, such as when individuals are automatically enrolled into retirement savings plans with contribution rates that automatically escalate over time.

---

[26] Joanne M. Miller and Jon A. Krosnick, "The Impact of Candidate Name Order on Election Outcomes," *Public Opinion Quarterly* 62 (1998): 291–330. As a corollary to this point, in situations where agencies offer many options and there is truly no evidence that one option or another is more appropriate for an individual or business, agencies should consider randomizing the order in which options are presented.

[27] See: https://www.healthcare.gov/choose-a-plan/plans-categories/; Peter A. Ubel, David A. Comerford, and Eric Johnson, "Healthcare.gov 3.0 — Behavioral Economics and Insurance Exchanges," *New England Journal of Medicine* 372 (2015): 695–698.

[28] Jeffrey R. Kling, Sendhil Mullainathan, Eldar Shafir, Lee Vermeulen, and Marian Wrobel, "Comparison Friction: Experimental Evidence from Medicare Drug Plans," *Quarterly Journal of Economics* 127 (2012): 199–235.

[29] See Richard H. Thaler and Will Tucker, "Smarter Information, Smarter Consumers," *Harvard Business Review* (January-February 2013).

[30] See Executive Order 13642 of May 9, 2013, "Making Open and Machine Readable the New Default for Government Information," and "Smart Disclosure and Consumer Decision Making: Report of the Task Force on Smart Disclosure," National Science and Technology Council (2013).

[31] Richard H. Thaler, Cass R. Sunstein, and John P. Balz, "Choice Architecture," in Eldar Shafir, ed., *The Behavioral Foundations of Public Policy*, (Princeton, 2012).

[32] Craig N. Smith, Daniel G. Goldstein, and Eric J. Johnson, "Smart Defaults: From Hidden Persuaders to Adaptive Helpers," INSEAD Business School Research Paper No. 2009/03/ISIC (2013); Yuting Zhang, Chao Zhou, and Seo Hyun Baik, "A Simple Change To The Medicare Part D Low-Income Subsidy Program Could Save $5 Billion," *Health Affairs* 33 (2014): 940–945.

[33] Benjamin R. Handel and Jonathan T. Kolstad, "Health Insurance for 'Humans': Information Frictions, Plan Choice, and Consumer Welfare," *American Economic Review* 105 (2015): 2449–2500; Saurabh Bhargava, George Loewenstein, Justin Sydnor, "Do Individuals Make Sensible Health Insurance Decisions? Evidence from a Menu with Dominated Options," (NBER Working Paper No. 21160, 2015); Eric J. Johnson, Ran Hassin, Tom Baker, Allison T. Bajger, and Galen Treuer, "Can Consumers Make Affordable Care Affordable? The Value of Choice Architecture," *PLoS ONE* 8 (2013): e81521.

In circumstances where defaults are not desirable or feasible, agencies should consider presenting individuals with active choices—that is, requiring or prompting individuals to make a choice in the absence of a default.[34] For example, asking workers to make an active choice about their participation in retirement savings plans has been shown to boost participation rates.[35]

Additional considerations may depend on the frequency with which choices are made. Special attention should be given to decisions individuals will make infrequently, especially those that are difficult to later change. Infrequent or irreversible choices provide few opportunities for individuals to learn from or revisit their decisions, increasing the stakes and justifying particularly careful attention to default settings. Where individuals are asked to make choices on a recurring basis, as with annual health-insurance open enrollment periods, program designers should be aware that individuals tend to stick with their earlier choices.[36]

Finally, it should be noted that defaults are not simply a useful tool for supporting good choices from among an existing set of options. Defaults can also be a powerful tool for introducing new program features, while preserving old ones. Program and policy reforms sometimes replace existing options. With defaults, agencies have the additional options of either introducing the new features as the default and leaving the older features as an available option, or retaining the old program features as the default and introducing new features as available options.

3.2.3. *Where programs offer many options, or options that differ in many ways, consider efforts to reduce the number and dimensionality of choices*

It should not be assumed that adding large numbers of program options, or allowing choices to vary along many dimensions, will necessarily lead to better outcomes for individuals. Presenting individuals with a large number of complex options can make optimal choosing difficult for individuals, and under some circumstances may lead individuals to avoid making a choice altogether.[37]

As a result, the underlying structure of program choices may benefit from simplification. Agencies should consider ways to standardize offerings or otherwise limit the dimensions along which options differ. This is true when distinctions are not necessary to fulfill core policy goals, or when the costs associated with presenting individuals with additional program features or a wider array of choices outweigh the benefits.[38] For example, while student-loan borrowers now have the option to choose from among at least four different, but similar, income-driven repayment plans (in addition to their standard repayment plan), a proposed reform would be to reduce this set to a single income-driven repayment option in order to simplify the choice.[39]

---

[34] Punam Anand Keller, Bari Harlam, George Loewenstein, and Kevin G. Volpp, "Enhanced Active Choice: A new Method to Motivate Behavior Change," *Journal of Consumer Psychology* 21 (2011): 376–383.

[35] Gabriel D. Carroll, James J. Choi, David Laibson, Brigitte Madrian, and Andrew Metrick, "Optimal Defaults and Active Decisions," *Quarterly Journal of Economics* 124 (2009): 1639–1676;

[36] William Samuelson and Richard Zeckhauser, "Status Quo Bias in Decision Making," *Journal of Risk and Uncertainty* 1(1988): 7–59.

[37] Sheena Iyengar, Gal Huberman, and Wei Jiang, "How Much Choice Is Too Much? Contributions to 401(k) Retirement Plans," in *Pension Design and Structure New Lessons from Behavioral Finance*, Olivia Mitchell and Stephen Utkus, eds. (Oxford, UK: Oxford University Press, 2004); Sheena Iyengar and Mark Lepper, "When Choice Is Demotivating: Can One Desire Too Much of a Good Thing?" *Journal of Personality and Social Psychology* 79 (2000): 995–1006; Alexander Chernev, Ulf Böckenholt, and Joseph Goodman, "Choice Overload: A Conceptual Review and Meta-Analysis," *Journal of Consumer Psychology* 25 (2015): 333–358.

[38] Saurabh Bhargava and George Loewenstein, "Choosing a Health Insurance Plan, Complexity and Consequences," *Journal of the American Medical Association*, 314 (2015): 2505–2506; Keith M. Marzilli Ericson and Amanda Starc, "How Product Standardization Affects Choice: Evidence from the Massachusetts Health Insurance Exchange," (NBER Working Paper No. 19527, October 2013).

[39] Department of Education, "Student Aid Overview: Fiscal Year 2017 Budget Request," (2016), p. 8. Available at: http://www2.ed.gov/about/overview/budget/budget17/justifications/n-sao.pdf

3.2.4.Where programs entail implicit choices, consider efforts to assist individuals with those decisions

Not all choices within programs entail explicit selections from menus of options at discrete points in time. Instead, many highly consequential choices are made implicitly, as part of ongoing interactions within programs. For example, workers covered by Social Security can claim retirement benefits at any time after reaching age 62. The choice of when to claim is implicit in the sense that individuals never face a single moment in time during which they are asked to select a claiming age. In these cases of implicit choice, all of the challenges associated with the presentation and structure of choices noted previously still apply.[40] Carefully considering how implicit choices are designed and how options and consequences are communicated to individuals can have significant impacts on program outcomes and individual welfare.

4. **Incentive design**

Finally, section (1)(b)(iv) of Executive Order 13707 encourages agencies to "review elements of their policies and programs that are designed to encourage or make it easier for Americans to take specific actions, such as saving for retirement or completing education programs. In doing so, agencies shall consider how the timing, frequency, presentation, and labeling of benefits, taxes, subsidies, and other incentives can more effectively and efficiently promote those actions, as appropriate. Particular attention should be paid to opportunities to use nonfinancial incentives."

Incentives are often used by agencies to encourage or discourage certain behaviors, practices, or market outcomes. For example, the Federal Government offers incentives for businesses that purchase energy efficient vehicles and use renewable fuels, hospitals that use electronic health records, and individuals who save for retirement.

When designing incentives, agencies should account for how individuals respond to both financial and nonfinancial incentives and consider the importance of the relative salience of those incentives, their timing, and their relationship to reference points.

4.1. Central insight: How individuals respond to financial incentives depends on the framing and structure of those incentives; individuals also respond to nonfinancial incentives

A central insight from behavioral science is that individuals do not respond to incentives as neatly as predicted by standard economic theory.[41] When financial incentives are used to encourage particular behaviors or advance particular policies, the amount, presentation, and structure of those incentives can influence their effectiveness. In addition, individuals respond, sometimes strongly, to non-price or non-financial incentives.[42]

4.2. Key implication: Agencies should consider efforts to enhance the effectiveness of program incentives

4.2.1.When utilizing financial incentives, consider the salience of the incentive

---

[40] Jeffrey B. Liebman and Erzo F. P. Luttmer, "Would People Behave Differently If They Better Understood Social Security? Evidence from a Field Experiment," *American Economic Journal Economic Policy* 7 (2015): 275–299; Jeffrey R. Brown, Arie Kapteyn, and Olivia S. Mitchell, "Framing and Claiming: How Information-Framing Affects Expected Social Security Claiming Behavior," *Journal of Risk and Insurance* 83 (2016): 139–162; Melissa A. Z. Knoll, Kirstin C. Appelt, Eric J. Johnson, & Jonathan E. Westfall, "Time to Retire: Why Americans Claim Benefits Early and How to Encourage Delay," *Behavioral Science and Policy* 53 (2015): 53–62.

[41] Emir Kamenica, "Behavioral Economics and Psychology of Incentives," *Annual Review of Economics* 4 (2012): 427–452; Uri Gneezy, Stephan Meier, and Pedro Rey-Biel, "When and Why Incentives (Don't) Work to Modify Behavior," *Journal of Economic Perspectives* 25 (2011): 191–210.

[42] Richard H. Thaler and Cass R. Sunstein, *Nudge* (Yale, 2008); Brigitte C. Madrian, "Applying Insights from Behavioral Economics to Policy Design," *Annual Review of Economics* 6 (2014): 663–688.

Standard economic theory suggests that individuals will react to a price increase by reducing their demand for an item (and conversely, react to a price decrease by increasing their demand for an item). Behavioral economics suggests that this relationship can be mediated by the degree to which prices are salient. For example, research suggests that consumers respond more strongly to changes in excise taxes, which are typically reflected in posted prices, than to changes in sales taxes, which are typically not displayed on price tags.[43]

In cases where the goal of an incentive is to encourage a particular behavior, agencies should ensure the incentive is salient to individuals. Incentives may be more salient if they are provided in isolation, rather than as part of a larger payment such as an income tax refund. Incentives may be less salient if they are embedded in otherwise complicated programs or schedules, such as the tax code.[44] Simple reminders can be an effective way to keep incentives salient.[45]

Finally, the salience of incentives can depend on the form or structure of the incentives. Research on the retirement savings contributions credit, or Saver's Credit, suggests that individuals may be more likely to respond to the incentive to save if the benefit were structured as a match to savings, rather than as a tax credit.[46]

4.2.2. *Consider the timing of incentives*

Immediate incentives are likely to be more effective than delayed incentives.[47] Agencies should consider factors such as whether individuals engage with incentives at the same time they take an action or only after a delay. Research finds, for example, that tax incentives for the purchase of hybrid vehicles are more effective at increasing the adoption of fuel-efficient cars when the customer receives the tax incentive at the point of purchase via a state sales tax waiver rather than as an income tax credit, which the customer receives when filing taxes, possibly months after the purchase.[48] Similarly, research shows that tax credits for households paying tuition and fees for education, which are received as part of the household's income tax refund long after an individual decides to attend school, have little impact on college attendance.[49]

[43] Raj Chetty, Adam Looney, and Kory Kroft, "Salience and Taxation: Theory and Evidence," *American Economic Review* 99 (2009): 1145–1177.

[44] Jeffrey B. Liebman and Richard J. Zeckhauser, "Schmeduling," (Harvard University Working Paper, 2004).

[45] John Guyton, Dayanand S. Manoli, Brenda Schafer, Michael Sebastiani, "Reminders & Recidivism: Evidence from Tax Filing & EITC Participation among Low-Income Nonfilers, (NBER Working Paper No. 21904, January 2016).

[46] Esther Duflo, William Gale, Jeffrey Liebman, Peter Orszag, Emmanuel Saez, "Saving Incentives for Low- and Middle-Income Families: Evidence from a Field Experiment with H&R Block," *Quarterly Journal of Economics* 121 (2006): 1311–1146; Emmanuel Saez, "Details Matter: The Impact of Presentation and Information on the Take-up of Financial Incentives for Retirement Saving," *American Economic Journal Economic Policy* 1 (2009): 204–228.

[47] Shane Frederick, George Loewenstein and Ted O'Donoghue, "Time Discounting and Time Preference: A Critical Review," *Journal of Economic Literature*, 40 (2002): 351–401.

[48] Kelly S. Gallagher and Erich Muehlegger, "Giving Green to Get Green? Incentives and Consumer Adoption of Hybrid Vehicle Technology," *Journal of Environmental Economics and Management* 61 (2011): 1–15.

[49] George B. Bulman and Caroline M. Hoxby, "The Returns to the Federal Tax Credits for Higher Education," *Tax Policy and the Economy* 29 (2015): 13–88.

4.2.3. Consider the reference points against which individuals may evaluate incentives when structuring and framing incentives

Standard economic models suggest that the only factor influencing an incentive's effectiveness is the size of the incentive—the larger the incentive, the larger its effect. Yet, behavioral science suggests that individuals evaluate incentives relative to a reference point, and even very small incentives can have a large impact on behavior. Individuals may be more likely to respond to an incentive that is framed as a loss rather than as a gain, even when the two incentives are the same monetary amount.[50] For example, a five-cent tax on disposable grocery bags led to a significant decrease in plastic-bag use; in contrast, a financially equivalent reward for reusable bag use had no effect.[51]

The impact of incentives on behavior also depends on how their levels change, if at all, relative to expectations, past payments, or other reference points. For example, behavioral economics research shows that an unemployment-insurance system that frontloads benefit amounts rather than holding them constant over time can help people to return to work more quickly.[52]

Finally, in part for these reasons, financial incentives can have unintended consequences. For example, while cost-sharing provisions in health-insurance programs are intended to serve as incentives to help curb overutilization, they can also contribute to the underutilization of valuable care.[53] In addition, when incentives are too modest they may fail to motivate the intended behavior; where disincentives are too modest they may even appear to license the behavior.[54]

4.2.4. Consider the use of nonfinancial incentives

Behavioral-science research shows that individuals respond to nonfinancial incentives; that is, there are design features of programs other than prices, taxes, or subsidies that can be implemented specifically to encourage or discourage particular behaviors. Research has now identified, and continues to refine, a toolkit of such approaches.[55] For example, in many contexts, individuals are motivated by social comparisons, such as learning about the behavior of their peers. Research finds that individuals reduce residential energy consumption when provided with information on how their consumption compares with that of their neighbors.[56] Similarly, social comparisons have been found to promote tax compliance.[57] To take another example of the impact of nonfinancial incentives, adding a signature confirmation to the top of forms (including online forms) on which individuals or businesses self-report

---

[50] Daniel Kahneman and Amos Tversky, "Prospect Theory: An Analysis of Decision under Risk," *Econometrica* 47 (1979): 263–291; Roland G. Fryer, Jr, Steven D. Levitt, John List, and Sally Sadoff, "Enhancing the Efficacy of Teacher Incentives through Loss Aversion: A Field Experiment," (NBER Working Paper No. 18237, 2012).

[51] Tatiana Homonoff, "Can Small Increases Have Large Effects? The Impact of Taxes versus Bonuses on Disposable Bag Use," (Princeton University Industrial Relations Section Working Paper No. 575, 2013).

[52] Stefano DellaVigna, Attila Lindner, Balázs Reizer, Johannes F. Schmieder, "Reference-Dependent Job Search: Evidence from Hungary," (NBER Working Paper No. 22257, May 2016).

[53] Katherine Baicker, Sendhil Mullainathan, and Joshua Schwartzstein, "Behavioral Hazard in Health Insurance," *Quarterly Journal of Economics* 130 (2015): 1623–1667

[54] Uri Gneezy and Aldo Rustichini, "Pay Enough or Don't Pay at All," *Quarterly Journal of Economics* 115 (2000): 791–810; Uri Gneezy and Aldo Rustichini, "A Fine Is a Price," *The Journal of Legal Studies* 29 (2000): 1–17.

[55] Brigitte C. Madrian, "Applying Insights from Behavioral Economics to Policy Design," *Annual Review of Economics* 6 (2014): 663–688.

[56] Hunt Allcott, "Social Norms and Energy Conservation," *Journal of Public Economics* 95 (2011): 1082–1095; Hunt Allcott and Todd Rogers, "The Short-Run and Long-Run Effects of Behavioral Interventions: Experimental Evidence from Energy Conservation," *American Economic Review* 104 (2014): 3003–3037; Paul J. Ferraro, Juan Jose Miranda, and Michael K. Price, "The Persistence of Treatment Effects with Norm-Based Policy Instruments: Evidence from a Randomized Environmental Policy Experiment," *American Economic Review* 101 (2011): 318–322.

[57] Michael Hallsworth, John A. List, Robert D. Metcalfe, and Ivo Vlaev, "The Behavioralist as Tax Collector: Using Natural Field Experiments to Enhance Tax Compliance," (NBER Working Paper No. 20007, 2014).

income, sales, or other data may promote greater accuracy in self-reports.[58] Planning prompts, which ask individuals to make specific plans to take an action, have been shown to effectively increase flu vaccination rates.[59]

4.2.5. *Consider the relative efficiency of financial and nonfinancial incentives*

Often, achieving a policy goal through the use of incentives entails paying individuals directly for engaging in a particular behavior, such as installing energy-efficient technologies in the home. When financial incentives are offered to individuals or businesses, those incentives may motivate behavior change by some of the targeted individuals. In other instances, incentives merely represent payments to individuals who would have engaged in the indicated behavior even without the incentive.

The total cost of motivating the indicated behavior, therefore, includes payments to individuals who would have engaged in the activity even without the payment. It is important to recognize this fact when designing incentives and when preparing cost-benefit analyses, and to compare the total costs to what could be achieved through the use of nonfinancial incentives. For example, research has compared alternative incentives for retirement savings, finding in one study that while tax benefits are expensive in terms of tax expenditures, they induce relatively little new retirement saving; on the other hand, automatic enrollment in those plans motivates new retirement saving at little direct cost to the government.[60]

---

[58] Lisa L. Shu, Nina Mazar, Francesca Gino, Dan Ariely, and Max H. Bazerman, "Signing at the Beginning Makes Ethics Salient and Decreases Dishonest Self-Reports in Comparison to Signing at the End," *Proceedings of the National Academy of Sciences* 109 (2012): 15197–15200.
[59] Katherine L. Milkman, John Beshears, James J. Choi, David Laibson, and Brigitte C. Madrian, "Using Implementation Intentions Prompts to Enhance Influenza Vaccination Rates," *Proceedings of the National Academy of Sciences,* 108 (2011):10415–10420.
[60] Raj Chetty, John N. Friedman, Søren Leth-Petersen, Torben Heien Nielsen and Tore Olsen, "Active vs. Passive Decisions and Crowd-Out in Retirement Savings Accounts: Evidence from Denmark," *Quarterly Journal of Economics* 129, (2014): 1141–1219.

www.ingramcontent.com/pod-product-compliance
Lightning Source LLC
Chambersburg PA
CBHW081748280526
45789CB00008B/2775